P9-DNN-599

IN LINCOLN'S HAND

Abraham Lincoln.

Four score and seven years ago our fath

ought forth, upon this continent, a new nation,

wed in Liberty, and dedicated to the propo

hat all men are created equal.

Now we are engaged in a great civil wa

g whether that nation, or any nation, so co

so dedicated, can long endure. We are

re on a great battlefield of that war.

at to dedicate a portion of it as the a final

g place of those who here gave their li

that nation might live. It is altogether

a proper that we should do this.

But in a larger sense we can not de

e can not consecrate — we can not hallow

round. The brave men, living and dead, w

led here, have consecrated it far above our

add or detract. The world will little

IN LINCOLN'S HAND

———— ⌘ ————

HIS ORIGINAL MANUSCRIPTS WITH

COMMENTARY BY DISTINGUISHED AMERICANS

· · ·

Edited by Harold Holzer and Joshua Wolf Shenk

Foreword by James H. Billington

BANTAM BOOKS

CREDITS

Cover image: Portrait made at Mathew Brady's gallery, April 20, 1864
Cover manuscript: The Second Inaugural Address, Library of Congress

MANUSCRIPTS

All manuscripts are reproduced from originals in the Robert Todd Lincoln Collection in the Manuscript Division of the Library of Congress, with the following exceptions:
4: This item is reproduced by permission of The Huntington Library, San Marino, California [HM 25119] **14:** Abraham Lincoln Presidential Library & Museum (ALPLM) **28:** Historical Society of Pennsylvania, Simon Gratz Collection **34:** Abraham Lincoln Presidential Library & Museum (ALPLM) **52:** Andre de Coppett Collection, Manuscripts Division, Department of Rare Books and Special Collections, Princeton University Library **54:** The Gilder Lehrman Collection, on deposit at the New York Historical Society, New York [GLC 5302] **56:** The Gilder Lehrman Collection, on deposit at the New York Historical Society, New York [GLC 2533] **96:** Wadsworth Atheneum Museum of Art, Hartford, CT. Gift of Miss Elizabeth Dixon **102:** Brown University Library **104:** Courtesy of the New York State Library Manuscripts and Special Collections Division **114:** Photograph courtesy of Christie's **124:** Abraham Lincoln Presidential Library & Museum (ALPLM) **130:** Brown University Library **138, 140:** The Alfred W. Stern Collection, Rare Book & Special Collections Division, Library of Congress **176 (top):** National Archives **176 (bottom):** Chicago History Museum (ICHi-30836)

IMAGES

For Library of Congress items, the following list provides the reproduction numbers.

Symbols used

P&P: Prints and Photographs Division
RBSC: Rare Book and Special Collections Division
PA: Performing Arts Division
SER: Serial & Government Publications Division
G&M: Geography and Map Division
GenColl: General Collections

ii: P&P, lc-dig-cph-3a53289 **x:** P&P, lc-dig-ppmsca-19206 **xii:** P&P, lc-dig-cph-3g02439 **7:** Abraham Lincoln Presidential Library and Museum (ALPLM) **9:** P&P, lc-dig-cwpbh-01588 **11:** P&P, LOT 5908 **13:** P&P, lc-dig-cph-3a14788 **17:** Abraham Lincoln Presidential Library & Museum (ALPLM) **21 (top):** PA, ML95H45 case box 3 p. 853 **21 (bottom):** SER, *Louisville Public Advertiser,* March 8, 1826 **23:** Abraham Lincoln Presidential Library & Museum (ALPLM) **25:** Lucy Speed, Mathew Harris Jouett, American, 1788-1827, Mrs. John Speed (nee Lucy Gilmer Fry), Oil on canvas, 26x21 inches, Gift of Mrs. Hattie Bishop Speed, 1942. Collection of the Speed Art Museum, Louisville, KY **26:** P&P, lc-dig-cph-3g02472 **27 (left):** P&P, lc-dig-ppmsca-18446 **27 (right):** P&P, lc-dig-cph-3a36988 **31:** Collection of Lincoln Financial Foundation (Ref #976) **33 (top, left and right):** RBSC, BS185 1833 .P48 **33 (middle):** RBSC, PR 4300 1815 .B2 **33 (bottom, left and right):** RBSC, PR 2753 .D65 1832 **37:** P&P, lc-dig-cph-3g06189 **39:** P&P, lc-dig-cph-3g03595 **43:** P&P, lc-dig-cph-3a17213 **45:** P&P, lc-dig-cph-3a13087 **47:** P&P, lc-dig-cph-3c32820 **48:** P&P, lc-dig-cph-3a12815 **53 (left):** P&P, lc-dig-cwpbh-00882 **53 (right):** P&P, lc-dig-cph-3a41326 **61:** P&P, lc-dig-cph-3a13881 **63 (top):** P&P, lc-dig-cph-3a16003 **63 (bottom):** Photograph Courtesy of the Abraham Lincoln Museum of Lincoln Memorial University, Harrogate, Tennessee **65:** P&P, lc-dig-cph-3a52060 **69 (left to right):** P&P, lc-dig-ppmsca-19246, lc-dig-ppmsca-19247, lc-dig-ppmsca-19248 **73 (top):** P&P, LC-dig-pga-01637 **73 (bottom):** P&P, LC-dig-cph-3b37029 **75:** P&P, lc-dig-cph-3a12815 **76 (top):** P&P, lc-dig-cph-3a33373 **76 (bottom):** Abraham Lincoln Presidential Library & Museum (ALPLM) **77 (top):** P&P, lc-dig-cph-3a32145 **77 (bottom):** P&P, lc-dig-cph-3a09984 **80:** P&P, lc-dig-cph-3a16525 **87:** P&P, lc-dig-cph-3c06731 **91:** A Great Rush, Collection of NY Historical Society, ac03148 **93 (top):** P&P, lc-dig-cph-3b52027 **93 (bottom):** P&P, lc-dig-cph-3a33416 **99:** P&P, lc-dig-cwpbh-00704 **101:** Lincoln as pharmacist, Collection of NY Historical Society, aj29043 **107 (top):** P&P, lc-dig-ppmsca-18444 **107 (bottom):** P&P, lc-dig-cph-3c00066 **109 (top):** P&P, LC-dig-cph-3a05783 **109 (bottom):** Miscenegation, Frank J. and Virginia Williams Collection **111:** P&P, lc-dig-pga-02797 **116:** P&P, lc-dig-ppmsca-07636 **117 (top):** RBSC, scsm0558 **117 (bottom):** P&P, lc-dig-pga-02502 **118:** P&P, lc-dig-ppmsca-18958 **123:** P&P, lc-dig-cph-3a14818 **125:** Collection of Lincoln Financial Foundation (Ref # 4051) **129 (top):** P&P, lc-dig-cwpbh-01194 **129 (bottom):** P&P, lc-dig-cph-3b35986 **131:** Lincoln Financial Collection (Ref # 4034) **135:** P&P, lc-dig-cph-3b15783 **141:** By permission of the Folger Shakespeare Library **145:** GenColl, Harper's Weekly, March 14, 1863 **147 (top):** James C. Conkling, Picture History **147 (bottom):** P&P, LOT 5908 **149:** P&P, lc-dig-cph-3b46046 **151 (top):** P&P, lc-dig-cph-3c32207 **151 (middle):** P&P, lc-dig-cph-3c32213 **151 (bottom):** P&P, lc-dig-cph-3c32209 **153:** P&P, lc-dig-pga-01949 **155:** G&M, g3701s cw0071c20 **157 (top):** P&P, lc-dig-cph-3b51331 **157 (middle):** P&P, Sketch of the Battle of Gettysburg by Edwin Forbes **157 (bottom):** P&P, lc-dig-cph-3b50007 **161:** P&P, lc-dig-cwpb-00383 **163:** P&P, lc-dig-ppmsca-17807 **165 (top):** P&P, lc-dig-cph-3c21302 **165 (bottom):** P&P, lc-dig-cwpb-07639 **173 (top):** P&P, lc-dig-cph-3b08069 **173 (bottom):** P&P, lc-dig-cph-3a18122 **174:** P&P, lc-dig-pga-01590 **175:** P&P, lc-dig-ppmsca-17562 **181:** Eliza Gurney, Picture History **183:** P&P, lc-dig-cph-3g01820 **187:** P&P, lc-dig-cph-3a06250 **189 (top):** P&P, lc-dig-cph-3a10740 **189 (bottom):** P&P, lc-dig-ppmsc-02928 **191 (top):** RBSC, scsm0515 **191 (bottom):** RBSC, scsm0830 **193 (top):** P&P, lc-dig-cph-3a14279 **193 (bottom):** GenColl, *London Illustrated News,* May 20, 1865

SPECIAL CREDITS

83: Commentary adapted with permission from Safire, William. *Safire's Political Dictionary.* New York: Oxford University Press, 2008. **163:** Commentary adapted with permission from Morrison, Toni. *Nobel Prize Acceptance Speech.* The Nobel Foundation. Nobel Banquet, Stockholm. 7 December 1993.

IN LINCOLN'S HAND
A Bantam Book / February 2009

Published by Bantam Dell
A Division of Random House, Inc. New York, New York

Library of Congress Cataloging-in-Publication Data
Lincoln, Abraham, 1809–1865.
[Selections. 2009. Bantam Dell]
In Lincoln's hand : his original manuscripts / with commentary by distinguished
Americans ; edited by Harold Holzer and Joshua Wolf Shenk ;
foreword by James H. Billington. p.   cm.
Official companion volume of the Library of Congress 2009 bicentennial
exhibition which will launch in Washington, D.C.
Includes bibliographical references.
ISBN 978-0-553-80742-4 (hardcover)
1. Lincoln, Abraham, 1809–1865—Manuscripts—Exhibitions.
2. Lincoln, Abraham, 1809–1865—Political and social views—Exhibitions.
3. Presidents—United States—Manuscripts—Exhibitions.
4. United States—Politics and government—1849–1877—Sources—Exhibitions.
5. Manuscripts, American—Exhibitions.   I. Holzer, Harold.
II. Shenk, Joshua Wolf.   III. Billington, James H.   IV. Title.
E457.92 2009b
973.7092—dc22
2008036674

Printed in the United States of America
Published simultaneously in Canada
www.bantamdell.com
RRW   10 9 8 7 6 5 4 3 2 1

ACKNOWLEDGMENTS

The editors are deeply grateful to the individuals and institutions whose contributions and guidance were indispensable to the development of this collection and its magnificent presentation on these pages.

At the Library of Congress, we sincerely thank Aimee Hess, W. Ralph Eubanks, and Abigail Colodner of the Publishing Office. Helena Zinkham, Phil Michel, Sarah Duke, and Barbara O. Natanson and her staff helped immensely, as did scanners Dominic Sergi and Ronnie Hawkins. We are also thankful to the organizers of the exhibition that inspired this book: Kimberli Curry, Cheryl Ann Regan, and above all the institution's peerless expert on the Library's Lincoln collection, John R. Sellers.

Many individual staff aides, advisors, and counselors across the country helped facilitate our document commentaries. We want to express our debt in particular to: Gerald Rafshoon, Lauren Gay, Skip Rutherford, Bruce Lindsay, Hannah Richert, David Goldberg, Jean Becker, Tim Goeglein, Kevin Sullivan, Kristie Macosko, Pat Souders, Molly Rowley, Gloria Loomis, Marc Liepis, Rosemary Shields, Lori Glazer, Kraig Smith, Mary Porcelli, and James Cornelius.

The support of the Abraham Lincoln Bicentennial Commission to the Library of Congress exhibition has been crucial, and we acknowledge Harold Holzer's cochairmen, Senator Richard Durbin and Congressman Ray LaHood, and executive director Eileen Mackevich, as well as Jennifer Rosenfeld, David Early, and the rest of the ALBC staff.

Thanks also go to our colleagues at Washington College and The Metropolitan Museum of Art for their support. And loving gratitude to our family and friends. Joshua Wolf Shenk would especially like to thank Richard L. Shenk for his strength and grace through his own fiery trial, and to his many caregivers at the University of Louisville Hospital, the University of Cincinnati Hospital, the Drake Center, and the Craig Hospital.

To our inimitable contributors, who summoned their own literary vision to engage with Lincoln's, we offer our admiration and profound appreciation.

Finally, we express special thanks to Martha Kaplan, for her help in arranging the project, and the team at Bantam Dell for bringing it to fruition, including designer Liney Li, Jessica Waters, Glen Edelstein, Kelly Chian, Maggie Hart, and above all our tireless and talented editor, John J. Flicker.

—H.H. and J.W.S.

CONTENTS

FOREWORD

"I claim not to have controlled events, but confess plainly that events have controlled me," Abraham Lincoln wrote in an 1864 letter to Albert Hodges, editor of Kentucky's *Frankfort Commonwealth*. These words can be found in Lincoln's hand in the Manuscript Division of the Library of Congress, along with 20,000 original letters, notes, and drafts written by and to Lincoln and donated to the Library by his son in 1923. The Library's Lincoln collection— one of the largest in the world—also includes 10,500 pieces of memorabilia, more than 10,000 digital records related to Lincoln's legal career, and such affecting articles as the contents of Lincoln's pockets on the night he was assassinated.

Lincoln's connection to the Library began in 1861, when he stood on the steps of the U.S. Capitol building—then the home of the Library of Congress—to be sworn in as the nation's sixteenth president. In the four years before his assassination he appointed two Librarians of Congress and charged 125 books to his Library account. Today, Lincoln quotations found throughout the Library's flagship building, opened in 1897, celebrate the influence "Father Abraham" has had on all Americans. So it is only fitting that the Library of Congress has joined with the Abraham Lincoln Bicentennial Commission to honor the 2009 bicentennial of Lincoln's birth with an exhibition and this companion book, a unique presentation of forty-some documents in Lincoln's own hand, chosen by Lincoln scholars Harold Holzer and Joshua Wolf Shenk.

In Lincoln's Hand brings us a richer understanding of the power of Lincoln's rhetoric. Many of Lincoln's speeches are imprinted on the public mind, but those polished works show nothing of his raw, unedited prose. The cross-outs, misspellings, and rewrites reproduced in this volume reveal not just his words, but also his thought process as he meticulously crafted what he wanted to say. The array of public figures who offer their insights in this book gives evidence of the wide range of individuals Lincoln's legacy continues to reach today. The exhibition on which this book is based, made possible by a generous donation from Union Pacific, will travel to Sacramento, Chicago, Omaha, Atlanta, and Indianapolis, and the book will travel even farther—into homes and libraries across the country and throughout the world. We hope this volume will move you to further explore Lincoln's life, and history in general, by visiting the Library in person, or online at www.loc.gov.

—James H. Billington
Librarian of Congress

INTRODUCTION

On June 28, 1862, President Abraham Lincoln drew a line in the sand. With the Union Army staggering into its second year of war, he told William H. Seward, his secretary of state, that the country needed 100,000 new troops to put down the rebellion. But however dire the military conditions, he left no doubt of his determination: "I expect to maintain this contest until

cording to the textual evidence, only then did he go back and insert into the text "until successful, or"— dramatically altering the meaning of the passage.

As we glimpse the original manuscript, we are thrust into a new intimacy with Lincoln's mind. We see him in motion—straining for precision, balancing grim determination with an allowance of opti-

successful, or till I die, or am conquered, or my term expires, or Congress or the country forsakes me."

This famous passage, like many of Lincoln's, is ubiquitous. Type it into Google and you will find hundreds of hits. And of course it is in all the collections of Lincoln's writings, and in the biographies, and the Civil War histories.

But a view of the original manuscript shows something surprising. It is not precisely what Lincoln wrote.

When the president put pen to paper, his message was originally rather more bleak: "I expect to maintain this contest till I die, or am conquered, or my term expires, or Congress or the country forsakes me." Ac-

mism. We see him thinking, revising, pleading. We see where he stopped to dip his pen in ink. We see, in the signature, how his hand brushed against the wet ink, giving his familiar "A. Lincoln" the look of a wet dog shaking off the rain.

For generations, Americans, and people all over the world, have sought to know Lincoln—not only to learn his story but to grapple with his character, his mind, even his soul. There are thousands of good approaches, from statues and abstract art to scholarly histories and anthologies of primary source material. But the real key to knowing Lincoln is his writing. Putting words on paper was not just a way of governing the nation and stoking the fires of democracy; it was, well before his days of power, a way of governing his mind and stoking the fires of his imagination. "Writing," he once declared, "the art of communicating thoughts to the mind through the eye, is the great invention of the world." As much as any figure in history, he put that invention to work. With his pen, he not only gave purpose and meaning to a time of profound conflict, but laid the principled foundation for a new nation that rose from it.

Of course, his writings are beyond familiar. They are a kind of civic scripture, constantly reproduced in texts and even etched in marble. The former make his words accessible. The latter infuses them with grandeur. But soon we forget to look at the original source of the writing. Archivists lock the doors to the vaults that hold the precious manuscripts, offering the public only a transcription or the scratchy black-and-white microfilm.

As writers on Lincoln, we have occasionally been granted access beyond those locked doors and have come away with great affection for the encounter that ensues. One is rarely alone with a Lincoln masterpiece, but usually in the company of a curator or librarian. With the document laid out on a table—

and a feeling of intense respect pervading the room—a conversation starts. One of us notices an insertion or emendation or the quality of the handwriting; another follows this thread and offers an overview of what the document does, or what it means, or where it comes from.

Thus was born an idea: What if we reproduced Lincoln's manuscripts using the best scanning and printing technologies to yield the most accurate color and texture? And what if we then asked great modern figures to offer a commentary on a document of their choosing? In that way, we could not only directly experience the life of Lincoln's manuscripts, but also show how his words continue to live.

Our commentators are writers, performers, and public servants. In this, they represent the three dimensions of Lincoln's literary work. His compositions were often consummated in their dramatic utterance; at other times, he followed a successful speech by translating it onto the page. What Edmund Wilson said was true: "Alone among American presidents, it is possible to imagine Lincoln, grown up in a different milieu, becoming a distinguished writer of a not merely political kind." That said, in his maturity, Lincoln *was* a political writer. He devoted nearly all his creative energy to matters of state—principally the subjects of freedom, unity, self-determination, and equal opportunity. And he invented an entirely new political vernacular, free of bombast, classical allusions, and rhetorical grandiosity. Lincoln wrote common words for the common man.

In Lincoln's Hand is by no means an authoritative anthology. It is by design selective and impressionistic—highlighting some forty poignant examples from among the thousands of manuscripts Lincoln produced. Some are correspondence—letters sent by mail, or by hand, or by telegraph. Others are manuscripts for speeches or letter drafts. (Revisions on a document often indicate it to be a draft that Lincoln eventually corrected.) Others are private notes meant for no one's eyes but Abraham Lincoln's own.

But like a lifelike portrait from only a few brushstrokes, these documents do paint a portrait of an elusive man. From his teenage doggerel to his melancholy confessions to his experiments with satire, poetry, and scientific inquiry, Part One offers a portrait of Lincoln as a young writer, testing form, sounding out rhythms, and mastering directness, precision, and imagery. In Part Two, we see Lincoln shake off the parochial interests of his young career and forcefully take on the great questions of freedom and democracy, even as he reckons with electoral failure. In Part Three, Lincoln's compositions become acts of state, as a divided nation hangs on his turns of phrase until the phrases themselves—in particular, those on

emancipation—change the nation. And in Part Four, a president made haggard by war, nearly driven from office, composes the masterpieces that articulate a new foundation for the nation that Lincoln had so poignantly declared "almost chosen."

Of course, the writing in this book casts light on Lincoln's life and character. But Lincoln also casts light on the making of literature and on its relationship to public life. Going back to an age of paper and ink, even the smallest stroke can show how, in the hands of an attentive master, language makes meaning. And going back to a time when the relentless spirit of the writer joined with the highest political office, we can remember how vital authentic expression is to honest governance. Even after he defined the American experiment and summoned its promise in the Gettysburg Address, Lincoln kept revising, moving commas, searching for the perfect word.

Though much maligned as an ignorant naïf on his arrival in Washington, Lincoln's literary powers did command respect. Whitman admired him. Emerson praised him. Tolstoy revered him. Harriet Beecher Stowe said that Lincoln's words were "worthy to be inscribed in letters of gold." Today, to respect what he did, we offer the opposite—a chance to see his words as he wrote them.

—Harold Holzer and Joshua Wolf Shenk

A NOTE ON THE TEXT: For document titles and dates, we have followed the conventions established in the *Collected Works of Abraham Lincoln,* edited by Roy P. Basler. And while Lincoln's punctuation followed the fashion of his time—for example, he used what looks like an underscore to mark both pauses and ends of sentences—we have mostly adopted modern standards for our transcriptions. Occasionally, we came across text that Lincoln crossed out and that we couldn't make out. These are indicated with question marks, struck-through, in brackets. Also, in several cases, document images have been enhanced to make them more readable.

Opposite: Abraham Lincoln poses on Sunday, August 9, 1863, the first sittee at Alexander Gardner's brand-new photography gallery in Washington.

Daguerreotype by Nicholas H. Shepherd, Springfield, Illinois, ca. 1846.

Part One

"A TENDENCY TO MELANCHOLLY"

1824-1854

Abraham Lincoln grew up among people for whom "work" meant raising crops, splitting rails, and hauling loads to the mill. Theirs was an oral culture. Stories flowed freely, but books were scarce, and most folks did not see their value. So when young Abe stole away to read or write, his cousin Dennis Hanks pronounced the customary judgment: "Lincoln was lazy—a very lazy man," Hanks said. "He was always reading—scribbling—writing—ciphering—writing poetry &c. &c."

As it turned out, what seemed lazy—developing his relationship to language—became young Lincoln's most essential work. When he struck out on his own, entering politics, studying law, and establishing himself in the literate communities of New Salem and Springfield, Illinois, Lincoln's writings ranged far and wide. Some scholars dismiss his nonpolitical productions—for example, his poetry, satire, and scientific meditations—as naive and unpracticed. Other observers see his personal notes—like his melancholy reflections on January 23, 1841—as fodder only for biographical detail.

But it was in this period that Lincoln adopted the work ethic of his youth—and the rhythms and intimacy of spoken language he grew up immersed in—and put them to service in crafting plain language that delivered a substantial message. In these early works, we can hear his voice and can feel his commitment to communicating with his audience. The works here show the writer as a young man. Before long, even Dennis Hanks was claiming credit for teaching his cousin to scribble with a "buzzards quillen."

This page from Lincoln's boyhood notebooks in Indiana—scholars date it from 1824,
when he was a teenager—is among the earliest known examples of his writing.
The ink is faded, but the lower left-hand corner (enlarged opposite) contains a memorable ditty.

Lincoln's first written words are, the scholars tell us, probably not original, one of those bits of schoolboy doggerel that nobody teaches and everyone learns (although no one has found one just like it; maybe the joke *is* his own). But more to the matter, they are a reminder of the single most important thing about the young Lincoln that we know: He loved to read and write. There is no greater divide in life than the one between kids for whom the experience of reading is a painful or tedious one, whose rewards are remote, if real, and those for whom the experience of reading and writing are addictive, entrancing, overwhelming, and so intense as to offer a new life of their own—those for whom the moment of learning to read begins a second life of letters as rich as the primary life of experience. Lincoln was as clear a case of the second kind of child, and man, as anyone who has ever lived. His hand and pen were the axis of his experience, even as he made his living, and his reputation, first from his body and later from his mouth. He lived to read, and the distaste that still shocks us a little in his attitude toward his father—that Tom wrote his name "blunderingly" still offended his steady-handed son years later—surely has its root in this simple cause. It wasn't that his father could barely read or write; it was that he failed to see the point of it for his son, couldn't see that it not only had what would have been called "pecuniary value" but life purpose. "His hand and pen"—more than his mind and voice, more even than his heart and soul—his hand and pen *are* Lincoln, the reading mind turning the page, the writing fingers adding to the sum of the world's words.

The irony, arresting and in a way poignant, is that Lincoln, a man of action—often murderous, uniquely decisive—was first of all a man of books and thoughts, and a rueful humorist of their inability to mend men's ways, including his own. He *would* be good, though, and God, or Providence, or Fate, or merely the contingencies of history—it took him a lifetime to make up his mind which it was to be, and perhaps he never did—alone knew when. ◄

Abraham Lincoln

his hand and pen
he will be good but
god knows When

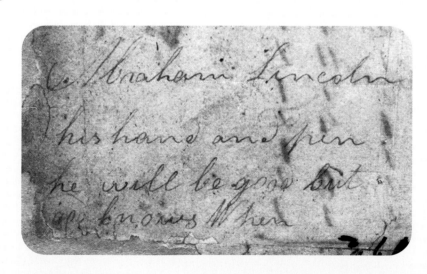

LETTER TO **ELIZA BROWNING**, APRIL 1, 1838

After a courtship gone badly awry with a young woman from Kentucky, Lincoln explained himself—
and satirized the whole affair—in a letter to his friend Eliza Browning.

Springfield, April 1. 1838

Dear Madam:

Without appologising for being egotistical, I shall make the history of so much of my own life, as has elapsed since I saw you, the subject of this letter— And by the way I now discover, that, in order to give a full and intelligible account of the things I have done and suffered since I saw you, I shall necessarily have to relate some that happened before—

It was, then, in the autumn of 1836, that a married lady of my acquaintance, and who was a great friend of mine, being about to pay a visit to her father and other relatives residing in Kentucky, proposed to me, that on her return she would bring a sister of hers with her, upon condition that I would engage to become her brother-in-law with all convenient dispatch— I, of course, accepted the proposal; for you know I could not have done otherwise, had I really been averse to it; but privately between you and me, I was most confoundedly well pleased with the project— I had seen the said sister some three years before, thought her intelligent and agreeable, and saw no good objection to plodding life through hand in hand with her— Time passed on, the lady took her journey, and in due time returned, sister in company sure enough— This stomached me a little; for it appeared to me, that her coming so readily showed that she was a trifle too willing; but on reflection it occured to me, that she might have been prevailed on by her married sister to come, without any thing concerning me ever

Springfield, April 1. 1838

Dear Madam:

Without appologising for being egotistical,
I shall make the history of so much of my own life, as has
elapsed since I saw you, the subject of this letter.
And by the way I now discover, that, in order to give
a full and inteligible account of the things I have done
and suffered <u>since</u> I saw you, I shall necessarily have
to relate some that happened <u>before</u>.

It was, then, in the autumn of 1836, that a married lady
of my acquaintance, and who was a great friend of mine, ~~who~~
being about to pay a visit to her father and other relatives
residing in Kentucky, proposed to me, that on her return she
would bring a sister of hers with her, upon condition that
I would engage to become her brother-in-law with all convenient dispach. I, of course, accepted the proposal; for you
know I could not have done otherwise, had I really been
averse to it; but privately between you and me, I was most
confoundedly well pleased with the project. I had seen the
said sister some three years before, thought her inteligent and
agreeable, and saw no good objection to plodding life through
hand in hand with her. Time passed on, the lady took her journey
and in due time returned, sister in company sure enough. This
stomached me a little; for it appeared to me, that her coming so
readily showed that she was a trifle too willing; but on reflection it occured to me, that she might have been prevailed on by
her married sister to come, without any thing concerning me ever

It's 1838. The twenty-six-year-old Charles Dickens has just published *Nicholas Nickleby*. Nikolai Gogol, a pointy-nosed twenty-nine-year-old Russian, is working on *Dead Souls*. What a generation! In Illinois, Lincoln, who is twenty-nine, pens—with almost no revision, it would appear—this comic gem.

In the space of a few lines, the subject of the letter, a Miss Mary Owens, goes from a fetching/slim/intelligent catch to a plus-sized, mother-suggesting bulk: wrinkle-free, yes, but only because so badly overstuffed. The humor is in the rapidity of this transformation. Miss Owens swells and grows homelier right in front of our eyes, as poor, tricked Abe stands there in her widening shadow, stovepipe hat in hand, contemplating his cheerless amorous future.

In truth, Owens was a beauty, if a little portly. She rejected Lincoln's marriage proposal because she felt he would be "deficient in those little links which make up the chain of woman's happiness," citing, among other things, the time he failed to carry a married woman's fat baby up a hill. Lincoln was bruised by her refusal; hence, perhaps, this savage, false, comic sketch of her, which he never expected to be made public.

A lesser writer (embarrassed, rejected), might have lingered too long on the riff of the Suddenly Repulsively Swelling Woman. But Lincoln turns his comic eye toward his own failings. This elevates the piece from satire to pathos. The story is suddenly sadder, a case study of human bumbling in the realm of the heart. ◀

having been mentioned to her; and so I concluded that
if no other objection presented itself, I would consent to
wave this — All this occurred upon my *hearing* of her arrival
in the neighbourhood; for, be it remembered, I had not yet
seen her, except about three years previous, as before mentioned —
In a few days, we had an interview, and although I
had seen her before, she did not look as my immagination
had pictured her — I knew she was over-size; but she
now appeared a fair match for Falstaff; I knew
she was called an "old maid", and I felt no doubt of
the truth of at least half of the appelation; but now,
when I beheld her, I could not for my life avoid thinking of my mother; and this, not from withered features,
for her skin was too full of fat, to permit its contracting
in to wrinkles; but from her want of teeth, weather-beaten
appearance in general, and from a kind of notion that ran in
my head, that nothing could have commenced at the size
of infancy, and reached her present bulk in less than thirty
five or forty years; and, in short, I was not all pleased
with her — But what could I do? I had told her sister that I would take her for better or for worse; and I
made a point of honor and conscience in all things, to
stick to my word, especially if others had been induced
to act on it, which in this case, I doubted not they had
for I was now fairly convinced, that no other man on earth
would have her, and hence the conclusion that they were
bent on holding me to my bargain — Well, thought I, I

having been mentioned to her; and so I concluded that

if no other objection presented itself, I would consent to

wave this. All this occured upon my <u>hearing</u> of her arrival

in the neighbourhood; for, be it remembered, I had not yet

<u>seen</u> her, except about three years previous, as before mentioned.

   In a few days we had an interview, and although I

had seen her before, she did ^not^ look as my immagination

had pictured her. I knew she was over-size, but she

now appeared a fair match for Falstaff; I knew

she was called an "old maid", and I felt no doubt of

the truth of at least half of the appelation; but now,

when I beheld her, I could not for my life avoid think-

ing of my mother; and this, not from withered features,

for her skin was too full of fat, to permit its contracting

in to wrinkles; but from her want of teeth, ~~and~~ weather-beaten

appearance in general, and from a kind of notion that ran in

my head, that <u>nothing</u> could have commenced at the size

of infancy, and reached her present bulk in less than thir-

tyfive or forty years; and, in short, I was not all pleased

with her. But what could I do? I had told her sis-

ter that I would take her for better or for worse; and I

made a point of honor and conscience in all things, to

stick to my word, especially if others had been induced

to act on it, which in this case, I doubted not they had,

for I was now fairly convinced, that no other man on earth

would have her, and hence the conclusion that they were

bent on holding me to my bargain. Well, thought I, I

Mary Owens remembered onetime suitor Lincoln as
"deficient in those little links which make up the chain of
a woman's happiness."

have said it, and, be consequences what they may, it
shall not be my fault if I fail to do it— At once I
determined to consider her my wife; and this done, all my
powers of discovery were put to the rack, in search of perfec=
tions in her, which might be fairly set-off against her defects— I tried
to immagine she was handsome, which, but for her unfortunate
corpulency, was actually true— Exclusive of this, no woman
that I have seen, has a finer face— I also tried to convince
myself, that the mind was much more to be valued than the
person; and in this, she was not inferior, as I could discover,
to any with whom I had been acquainted—

Shortly after this, without attempting to come to any positive un=
derstanding with her, I set out for Vandalia, where and when
you first saw me— During my stay there, I had letters from
her, which did not change my opinion of either her intellect
or intention; but on the contrary, confirmed it in both—
All this while, although I was, fixed "firm as the surge repell=
ing rock" in my resolution, I found I was continually repent=
ing the rashness, which had led me to make it— Through life
I have been in no bondage, either real or immaginary, from
the thraldom of which I so much desired to be free—
After my return home, I saw nothing to change my opin=
ion of her in any particular— She was the same and so
was I— I now spent my time between, planning how I might get
along through life after my contemplated change of
circumstances should have taken place; and how I might
procrastinate the evil day for a time, which I really dreaded
as much— perhaps more, than an irishman does the halter—

have said it, and, be consequences what they may, it

shall not be my fault if I fail to do it. At once I

determined to consider her my wife; and this done, all my

powers of discovery were put to the rack, in search of perfec-
      in her,   against
tions ^ which might be fairly set-off ~~to~~   her defects. I tried

to immagine she was handsome, which, but for her unfortunate

corpulency, was actually true. Exclusive of this, no woman

that I have seen, has a finer face. I also tried to convince

myself, that the mind was much more to be valued than the

person; and in this, she was not inferior, as I could discover,

to any with whom I had been acquainted.

    Shortly after this, without attempting to come to any positive un-

derstanding with her, I set out for Vandalia, where and when

you first saw me. During my stay there, I had letters from

her, which did not change my opinion of either her intelect

or intention; but on the contrary, confirmed it in both.

All this while, although I was fixed "firm as the surge repell-

ing rock" in my resolution, I found I was continually repent-

ing the rashness, which had led me to make it. Through life

I have been in no bondage, either real or immaginary from

the thraldom of which I so much desired to be free.

  After my return home, I saw nothing to change my opin-

ion of her in any particular. She was the same and so
                between
was I. I now spent my time [??] planing how I might get

along through life ~~when~~ after my contemplated change of

circumstances should have taken place; and how I might

procrastinate the evil day for a time, which I really dreaded

as [???] much — perhaps more, than an irishman does the halter.

Lincoln's longtime Illinois political ally Orville Hickman Browning had the distinction of losing an election to Democrat Stephen A. Douglas fourteen years before Lincoln did the same in his 1858 quest for the U.S. Senate. Browning became Lincoln's trusted advisor, even though he did not support him for the 1860 presidential nomination.

After all my suffering upon this deeply interest=
ing subject, here I am, wholly unexpectedly, complete=
ly out of the "scrape"; and I now want to know, if you
can guess how I got out of it — Out clear in every
sense of the term; no violation of word, honor or con=
science — I dont believe you can guess, and so I
may as well tell you at once — As the lawyers say, it
was done in the manner following, towit — After I
had delayed the matter as long as I thought I could
in honor do, which by the way, had brought me round into the
last fall, I concluded I might as well bring it to a
consummation without further delay; and so I mustered my.
resolution, and made the proposal to her direct; but, shocking
to relate, she answered, No — At first I supposed she
did it through an affectation of modesty, which I thought
but ill-become her, under the peculiar circumstances of her
case; but on my renewal of the charge, I found she repelled
it with greater firmness than before — I tried it again
and again, but with the same success, or rather with
the same want of success — I finally was forced
to give it up, at which I very unexpectedly found
myself mortified almost beyond endurance — I was
mortified, it seemed to me, in a hundred different
ways — ~~I tried so for the first time by~~ My vanity was
deeply wounded by the reflection, that I had so
long been too stupid to discover her intentions, and
at the same time never doubting that I understood them
perfectly; and also, that she whom I had taught my=

After all my suffering upon this deeply interest-

ing subject, here I am, wholly unexpectedly, complete-

ly out of the "scrape"; and I ^ now want to know, if you

can guess how I got out of it. Out clear in every

sense of the ^ term; ~~word~~; no violation of word, honor or con-

science. I dont believe you can guess, and so I

may as well tell you at once. As the lawyers say, it

was done in the manner following, towit. After I

had delayed the matter as long as I thought I could

in honor do, which by the way ^ had brought me round into the

last fall, I concluded I might as well bring it to a

consumation without further delay; and so I mustered my

resolution, and made the proposal to her direct; but, shocking

to relate, she answered, no. At first I supposed she

did it through an affectation of modesty, which I thought

but ill-become her, under the peculiar circumstances of her

case; but on my renewal of the charge, I found she repeled

it with greater firmness than before. I tried it again

and again, but with the same success, or rather with

the same want of success. I finally was forced

to give it up, at which I verry unexpectedly found

myself mortified almost beyond endurance. I was

mortified, it seemed to me, in a hundred different

ways. ~~I [????] for the first time began~~ My vanity was

deeply wounded by the reflection, that I had so

long been too stupid to discover her intentions, and

at the same time never doubting that I understood them

perfectly; and also, that she whom I had taught my-

Although he resolved in this letter "never again to think of marrying," Abraham Lincoln wed Mary Todd in this imposing Springfield mansion on November 4, 1842. The house belonged to her sister, Elizabeth Todd Edwards. Here, nearly forty years later, on July 15, 1882, the president's widow died.

self to believe nobody else would have, had actually
rejected me with all my fancied greatness; and to cap
the whole, I then, for the first time, began to suspect
that I was, really a little in love with her —— But let it
all go— I'll try and out live it— Others have been
made fools of by the girls; but this can never be with
truth said of me —— I most emphatically, in this in-
stance, made a fool of myself—— I have now come
to the conclusion never again to think of marrying; and for
this reason; I can never be satisfied with any one who
would be block-head enough to have me——

When you receive this, write me a long yarn about
something to amuse me— Give my respects to Mrs
Browning——

Your sincere friend
A. Lincoln

Mrs O. H. Browning ——

self to believe no body else would have, had actually

rejected me with all my fancied greatness; and to cap

the whole, I then, for the first time, began to suspect

that I was ^really a little in love with her. But let it

all go. I'll try and out live it. Others have been

made fools of by the girls; but this can never be with

truth said of me. I most emphatically, in this in-

stance, made a fool of myself. I have now come

to the conclusion never ^again to think of marrying; and for

this reason; I can never be satisfied with any one who

would be block-head enough to have me.

When you receive this, write me a long yarn about

something to amuse me. Give my respects to Mr.

Browning.

Your sincere friend

A. Lincoln

Mrs. O. H. Browning

Describing Springfield as a "busy wilderness" after he moved to
the new state capital in 1837—one of its muddy streets is
shown here in an early photo—Lincoln admitted he felt "quite
as lonesome here as I ever was anywhere in my life."

With his senior law partner at Congress in Washington, Lincoln was tasked to send regular updates on the political scene. But on this grim winter's day, his mind was in such "deplorable" shape that his depression—perhaps the worst spell in a life of melancholy—became the main topic.

Jany 23rd 1841- Springfield, Ills.

Dear Stuart:

Yours of the 3rd Inst is recd &
I proceed to answer it as well as I can, tho,
from the deplorable state of my mind at this
time. I fear I shall give you but little satisfaction.
About the matter of the Congressional election, I
can only tell you, that there is a bill now
before the Senate adopting the General Ticket
system; but whether the party have fully de=
termined on its adoption is yet uncertain —
There is no sign of opposition to you among our friends,
and none that I can learn among our enemies; tho.,
of course, there will be, if the Genl Ticket be
adopted — The Chicago American, Peoria Register, &
Sangamo Journal, had have already hoisted your flag
upon their own responsibility; & the other whig papers
of the District are expected to follow immediately.—
On last evening there was a meeting of our friends
at Butlers; and I submitted the question to them
& found them unanimously in favor of having you
announced as a candidate — A few of us this morning,
however, concluded, that as you were already being an=
nounced in the papers, we would delay announcing you,
& by your own authority for a week or two — We

Jany. 23rd 1841- Springfield, Ills.

Dear Stuart:

Yours of the 3rd Inst is recd &

I proceed to answer it as well as I can, tho,

from the deplorable state of my mind at this

time, I fear I shall give you but little satisfaction.

About the matter of the congressional election, I

can only tell you, that there is a bill now

before the Senate adopting the General Ticket

system; but whether the party have fully de-

termined on it's adoption is yet uncertain.

There is no sign of opposition to you among our friends;

and none that I can learn among our enemies; tho',

of course, there will be, if the Genl Ticket be

adopted. The Chicago American, Peoria Register, &

Sangamo Journal, ~~had~~ have already hoisted your flag

upon their own responsibility; & the other whig papers

of the District are expected to follow immediately.

On last evening there was a meeting of our friends

at Butler's; and I submitted the question to them

& found them unanamously in favour of having you

announced as a candidate. A few of us this morning,

however, concluded, that as you were already being an-

nounced in the papers, we would delay announcing you,

as by your own authority for a week or two. We

The signs of depression in this letter are reassuringly evocative of the definitional ones cataloged in modern diagnostic manuals. All depressives think that no one else has borne such pain as they know. All believe that they will never get better, that their agony is intransient. Depressed people believe that they are doing all they can to keep up with the basic business of their daily lives and cannot—as Lincoln would have it—write more. Lincoln asserts that he must get better or die, and that he does not believe he will get better; most depressives experience their despondency as mortal. Depression is in general an illness of self-obsession, and for all the dutiful rundown of the letter's ostensible purpose in the opening paragraph, Lincoln's real energy is devoted to narrating his own pain. What is particularly striking here, however, is that the thirty-one-year-old Lincoln does not assign any external cause for his depression.

Clinical depression tends to attach to external circumstances, so that it usually appears to have triggers even when it is essentially endogenous. But while many depressed people are distraught at the tiniest imperfections in their own lives, Lincoln manages in the end to be distraught about the human price paid by a nation facing its sorest test. There is a fallacy in circulation that depression is necessarily correlated with dysfunction, but more recent research has emphasized that there is such a thing as high-functioning depression, in which people are afflicted with the paralytic sensations of emotional deadness, isolation, and sorrow without the paralysis itself. Lincoln had the world's highest-functioning depression; weighted down, he contrived to lead a divided country through some of its darkest hours.

(continued)

thought that to appear too keen about it
might spur our opponents on about their Genl
Ticket project— Upon the whole, I think I
may say with certainty, that your re-election
is sure, if it be in the power of the whigs
to make it so—

For not giving you a general summary of news, you
must pardon me; it is not in my power to do
so— I am now the most miserable man living—
If what I feel were equally distributed to the
whole human family, there would not be one cheerful face on the earth— Whether I shall ever be
better I can not tell; I awfully forebode I shall
not— To remain as I am is impossible; I must die or
be better, it appears to me— The matter you speak
of on my account, you may attend to as you say, unless you
shall hear of my condition forbidding it— I say this, because I fear I shall be unable to attend to any
business here, and a change of scene might help me—
If I could be myself, I would rather remain
at home with Judge Logan— I can write no more.

                    Your friend, as ever—
                         A. Lincoln

thought that to appear too keen about it
might spur our opponents on about their Genl.
Ticket project. Upon the whole, I think I
may say with certainty, that your reelection
is sure, if it be in the power of the whigs
to make it so.

For not giving you a general summary of news, you
<u>must</u> pardon me; it is not in my power to do
so. I am now the most miserable man living.
If what I feel were equally distributed to the
whole human family, there would not be one cheerful face on the earth. Whether I shall ever be
better I can not tell; I awfully forebode I shall
not. To remain as I am is impossible; I must die or
be better, it appears to me. The matter you speak
of on my account, you may attend to as you say, unless you
shall hear of my condition forbidding it. I say this, because I fear I shall be unable to attend to any
bussiness here, and a change of scene might help me.
If I could be myself, I would rather remain
at home with Judge Logan. I can write no more.

Your friend, as ever —

A. Lincoln

It is almost as though Lincoln, having been afflicted early in his life by desolation without a cause and failing to mitigate it, ultimately found sufficient cause for it in the terrible war for the union in which he so devoutly believed. Today, a diagnosis of depression is considered sufficient to invalidate anyone's presidential campaign. We have spent years in a great war led by a president without any capacity for misery such as this, and his absence of a depressive response seems far more mad than the clinical syndrome portrayed in Lincoln's correspondence. War warrants despair, and the despair that can locate a just war on which to drape itself is the constructive basis not only for deep humanity, but also for great leadership, even for wisdom. ◄

Few men had more impact on Lincoln's early life than John Todd Stuart. The Whig attorney encouraged Lincoln to study law, lent him books, then took him into his practice as a partner. Stuart was also the cousin of Lincoln's future wife, Mary Todd.

Lincoln wrote to the half sister of his closest friend, Joshua Fry Speed, shortly after a long stay on their
family estate in Louisville. His narration of an encounter with a group of shackled slaves on the Ohio River
has long intrigued scholars, and fueled arguments on all sides.

Bloomington, Illinois, Sept 27th 1841

Miss Mary Speed
  Louisville, Ky
        My Friend:
              Having resolved to write
to some of your Mother's family, and not having
the express permission of any one of them do so,
I have had some little difficulty in determining
on which to inflict the task of reading what I
now feel must be a most dull and silly
letter; but when I remembered that you and
I were something of cronies while I was at Farmington, and that, while there, I once was under
the necessity of shutting you up in a room to
prevent your committing an assault and battery
upon me, I instantly decided that you should
be the devoted one.—

              I assume that you have not heard from
Joshua & myself since we left, because I think
it doubtful whether he has written—

              You remember there was some uneasiness about
Joshua's health when we left. That little indispo-
sition of his turned out to be nothing serious, and
it was pretty nearly forgotten when we reached
Springfield. We got on board the Steam Boat
Lebanon, in the Locks of the Canal about 12
o'clock M. of the day we left, and reached

Bloomington, Illinois, Sept 27th 1841

Miss Mary Speed

Louisville, Ky

My Friend:

Having resolved to write
to some of your Mother's family, and not having
the express permission of any one of them do so,
I have had some little difficulty in determining
on which to inflict the task of reading what I
now feel must be a most dull and silly
letter; but when I remembered that you and
I were something of cronies while I was at Farmington, and that, while there, I once was under
the necessity of shutting you up in a room to
prevent your committing an assault and battery
upon me, I instantly decided that you should
be the devoted one.

I assume that you have not heard from
Joshua & myself since we left, because I think
it doubtful whether he has written.

You remember there was some uneasiness about
Joshua's health when we left. That little indispo-
sition of his turned out to be nothing serious; and
it was pretty nearly forgotten when we reached
Springfield. We got on board the Steam Boat
Lebanon, in the locks of the Canal about 12
o,clock Pm. of the day we left, and reached

E. L. DOCTOROW

Having broken his engagement to Mary Todd in a rather cowardly way and then deciding that he loved her after all, the thirty-two-year-old Lincoln fell into a serious depression. He repaired to the Kentucky plantation of his close friend Joshua Speed, where, after a month, his spirits were somewhat restored. In this letter to Joshua's half sister, written upon his return to Illinois, Lincoln begins playfully, which suggests how well he could get along with women who were not thinking to marry him. He asks to be remembered one way or another to various females, old and young, as if, with his visit to the Speeds, he has found a surrogate family. His wait-and-see remark about the Bible as a cure for his "Blues" indicates his lifelong ambivalence about doctrinal religion, and his account of the chained but cheerful slaves on the Steamboat *Lebanon* reveals a certain lingering gloominess. Is he comparing their fate favorably to his own? The entire passage is ambiguous. Is he the Northerner admiring the slaves' fortitude or the Southerner noting their incomprehension? In any event it is disturbing to read, in his own hand, the future president's description of slaves as cheerful and happy: We think how torturous is moral progress when even the greatest mind of the age may be reflecting the ideology of the very system it finds abhorrent. ◄

St. Louis the next Monday at 8 P.M. —
Nothing of interest happened during this passage, except the vexatious delays occasioned by the sand
bars be thought interesting. — By the way, a fine
example was presented on board the boat for contemplating the effect of condition upon human happiness.
A gentleman had purchased twelve negroes in different
parts of Kentucky and was taking them to a farm in
the South. They were chained six and six together. — A small iron clevis was around the left
wrist of each, and this fastened to the main
chain by a shorter one at a convenient distance from the others; so
that the negroes were strung together precisely like
so many fish upon a trot-line. — In this condition
they were being seperated forever from the scenes
of their childhood, their friends, their fathers
and mothers, and brothers and sisters, and
many of them, from their wives and children,
and going into perpetual slavery where the
lash of the master is proverbially more ruthless
and unrelenting than any other where; and yet
amid all these distressing circumstances, as we would
think them, they were the most cheerful and ap-
parantly happy creatures on board. One, whose
offence for which he had been sold was an
over-fondness for his wife, played the fiddle

St. Louis the next Monday at 8 P.M.

Nothing of interest happened during the passage, except the vexatious delays occasioned by the sand

bars be thought interesting. By the way, a fine

example was presented on board the boat for contem-

plating the effect of <u>condition</u> upon human happiness.

A gentleman had purchased twelve negroes in diferent

parts of Kentucky and was taking ^ them to a farm in

the South. They were chained six and six toge-

ther. A small iron clevis was around the left

wrist of each, and this fastened to the main

chain ^ by a shorter one at a convenient ^ distance ~~distant~~ from the others; so

that the negroes were strung together precisely like

so many fish upon a trot-line. In this condition

they were being separated forever from the scenes

of their childhood, their friends, their fathers

and mothers, and brothers and sisters, and

many of them, from their wives and children,

and going into perpetual slavery where the

lash of the master is proverbially more ruthless

and unrelenting than any other where; and yet

amid all these distressing circumstances, as we would

think them, they were the most cheerful and ap-

parantly happy creatures on board. One, whose

offence for which he had been sold was an

over-fondness for his wife, played the fiddle

Lincoln made an extended visit to Farmington, the gracious Speed family
estate near Louisville, in August and September, 1841.

gant assortment ol PIANO FORTES, which he
offers for sale at the Philadelphia prices, with the
addition of charges from thence   Inquire of Mr.
I. Thom.   march 8—774ow

RAN AWAY

From the subscriber, living on
Bear Grass, five miles from
Louisville, a negro man, named
CHARLES,
commonly called Charles Harrison. He is about the common
size, with rather a yellowish
hue in the face, has a fine slick
skin, his eyes showing a good deal of the white, and
about 28 or 30 years old. He is a very intelligent
fellow, and remarkably handy; being a shoema-
ker, working mostly with pegs, preferring to make
pegged shoes, and does very good work. He is an
excellent gardener—very handy at butchering—
can lay brick, &c It is apprehended that he will
make for Indiana or Ohio. Very probably he may
attempt to get a passage in a steam boat.
  For the apprehension and security of said fellow, so that I get him, I will give, (if taken in
Kentucky,) fifty dollars. If taken on the north
side of the Ohio, and in like manner secured, I
will give to the person or persons so apprehending
and securing him, the sum of one hundred dollars.
                              JOHN SPEED.
  march 8—774ow

The Speed homestead relied on slave labor and, as
this newspaper advertisement indicates, the family
pursued its runaway "property" relentlessly.

21

almost continually; and the others danced, sung, cracked jokes, and played various games with cards from day to day— How true it is that "God tempers the wind to the shorn lamb," or in other words, that He renders the worst of human conditions tolerable, while He permits the best, to be nothing better than tolerable—

To return to the narative. When we reach= ed Springfield, I staid but one day when I started on this tedious circuit where I now am— Do you remember my going to the city while I was in Kentucky, to have a tooth extract= ed, and making a failure of it? Well, that same old tooth got to paining me so much, that about a week since I had it torn out, bringing with it a bit of the jaw= bone; the consequence of which is that my mouth is now so sore that I can nei= ther talk, nor eat— I am litterally "subsis= ting on savoury remembrances"— that is, being un= able to eat, I am living upon the remembrance of the delicious dishes, of peaches and cream we used to have at your house—

When we left, Miss Fanny Henning was owing you a visit, as I understood— Has she almost continually; and the others danced, sung, cracked jokes, and played various games with cards from day to day. How true it is that "God tempers the wind to the shorn lamb," or in other words, that He renders the worst of human conditions tolerable, while He permits the best, to be nothing better than tolerable.

To return to the narrative. When we reached Springfield, I staid but one day when I started on this tedious circuit where I now am. Do you remember my going to the city while I was in Kentucky, to have a tooth extracted, and making a failure of it? Well, that same old tooth got to paining me so much, that about a week since I had it torn out, bringing with it a bit of the jawbone; the consequence of which is that my mouth is now so sore that I can neither talk nor eat. I am litterally "subsisting on savoury remembrances" — that is, being unable to eat, I am living upon the remembrance of the delicious dishes of peaches and cream we used to have at your house.

When we left, Miss Fanny Henning was owing you a visit, as I understood. Has she

Lincoln's Springfield roommate, Joshua Fry Speed, was the best friend the future president ever had. Though Speed opposed Lincoln in the election of 1860, he became a crucial Union ally in wartime Kentucky.

paid it yet? If she has are you not convinced that she is one of the sweetest girls
in the world? There is but one thing about her,
so far as I could perceive, that I would have
otherwise than as it is— That is something of a
tendency to melancholy— This, let it be observed,
is a misfortune, not a fault— Give her an assurance
of my very highest regard, when you see her—

Is little Sip Eliza Davis at your house
yet? If she is, kiss her "over and over again" for me—

Tell your mother that I have not "got" her
"present" with me; but that I intend to
read it regularly when I return home. I
doubt not that it is really, as she says,
the best cure for the "Blues" could one
but take it according to the truth—

Give my respects to all your sisters (including
"Aunt Emma") and brother— Tell Mrs Peay,
of whose happy face I shall long retain a
pleasant remembrance, that I have been
trying to think of a name for her homestead,
but, as yet, can not satisfy myself with
one— I shall be very happy to receive a line
from you, soon after you receive this; and, in case
you choose to favor me with one, address it to
Charleston, Coles Co. Ills as I shall be there about
the time to receive it—

Your sincere friend,
A. Lincoln

paid it yet? If she has, are you not convinced that she is one of the sweetest girls
in the world? There is but one thing about her,
so far as I could perceive, that I would have
otherwise than as it is. That is something of a
tendency to melancholly. This, let it be observed,
is a misfortune, not a fault. Give her an assurance
of my very highest regard, when you see her.

　　　Is little Siss Eliza Davis at your house
yet? If she is, kiss her "o,er and o,er again" for me.
Tell your mother that I have not got her
"present" with me; but that I intend to
read it regularly when I return home. I
doubt not that it is really, as she says,
the best cure for the "Blues" could one
but take it according to the truth.
Give my respects to all your sisters (including
"Aunt Emma") and brothers. Tell Mrs. Peay,
of whose happy face I shall long retain a
pleasant remembrance, that I have been
trying to think of a name for her homestead,
but, as yet, can not satisfy myself with
one. I shall be very happy to receive a line
from you, soon after you receive this; and, in case
you choose to favour me with one, address it to
Charleston, Coles Co., Ills as I shall be there about
the time to receive it.　　Your sincere friend

A. Lincoln

Twenty years after he wrote this letter, President Lincoln
inscribed his photograph to the woman in this portrait, the
"pious" Lucy Speed, still fondly recalling the Bible she had
given him back in 1841.

Generations of illustrators showed Lincoln performing manual labor on the prairie—a book never far from his side.

Though Lincoln thought this 1857 photograph "a true one," his fastidious wife loathed it—"owing to the disordered condition of the hair," its subject admitted. But after the 1860 convention, printmakers resurrected it because it fit the developing image of the rough-hewn, self-made man.

e antislavery artist Eastman Johnson created this iconic portrait of the boy Lincoln studying by firelight in his yhood home.

LETTER TO **ANDREW JOHNSTON**, INCLUDING POEM, SEPTEMBER 6, 1846
An avid reader of poetry, Lincoln tried his hand at verse too. Here he sets up and delivers
the second of a three-part effort to his literary friend Andrew Johnston, who would arrange to publish the
lines in the Quincy *Whig*. Lincoln thought enough of his poem to allow publication—
but asked that it be made anonymous.

Springfield, Sept 6th 1846

"Friend Johnson:

You remember when I wrote you from Tremont last
spring sending you a little canto of what I called poetry, & promised to bore you with another some time— I now fulfil the
promise— The subject of the present one is an insane man— His
name is Matthew Gentry— He is three years older than I, and
when we were boys we went to school together— He was rather a bright lad, and the son of the rich man of our very
poor neighbourhood— At the age of nineteen he unaccountably
became furiously mad, from which condition he gradually settled
down into harmless insanity— When, as I told you in my other
letter I visited my old home in the fall of 1844, I found
him still lingering in this wretched condition— In my poetizing mood
I could not forget the impressions his case made upon me— Here
is the result—

> But here's an object more of dread
> Then aught the grave contains—
> A human form with reason fled,
> While wretched life remains—
>
> Poor Matthew! Once of genius bright,
> A fortune-favored child—
> Now locked for aye, in mental night,
> A haggard mad-man wild—

Springfield, Sept 6th 1846

Friend Johnson:

You remember when I wrote you from Fremont last spring, sending you a little canto of what I called poetry, I promised to bore you with another some time. I now fulfil the promise. The subject of the present one is an insane man. His name is Matthew Gentry. He is three years older than I, and when we were boys we went to school together. He was rather a bright lad, and the son of the rich man of our very poor neighbourhood. At the age of nineteen he unaccountably became furiously mad, from which condition he gradually settled down into harmless insanity. When, as I told you in my other letter I visited my old home in the fall of 1844, I found him still lingering in this wretched condition. In my poetizing mood I could not forget the impressions his case made upon me. Here is the result.

But here's an object more of dread
   Than ought the grave contains.
A human form with reason fled,
   While wretched life remains.

Poor Matthew! Once of genius bright,
   A fortune-favored child.
Now locked for aye, in mental night,
   A haggard mad-man wild.

Abraham Lincoln's poem "My Childhood Home I See Again" begins with the conventional nostalgia the title implies. The lines, at first merely adept, proceed from that nostalgia to elegy and then beyond elegy to a distinctly less conventional treatment of mortality: So many have died since the poet was last in Indiana that he feels that—with a shock of plain language as appears so often in Lincoln's prose—"I'm living in the tombs."

That unsettling phrase leads to "But here's an object more of dread." The "object" involves the mystery of a promising life that devolves into violent insanity and, after that horror, song: song of a terrible beauty, followed by bleak silence.

This "canto" (Lincoln's term) concerns his childhood schoolmate Matthew Gentry (like Lincoln, "rather a bright lad," and unlike Lincoln, from a well-off family). As Matthew's life story departs from comfortable expectation into homicidal, self-maiming rage, imploring grief, and absolute loss, Lincoln's verses also change from expert ballad stanzas to something far less comfortable. Imprisoned, Matthew sings. Lincoln recalls feeling drawn to that "sweet and lone" singing: "the funeral dirge, it ever seemed / Of reason dead and gone."

(continued)

Poor Matthew! I have ne'er forgot,
    When first, with maddened will,
Yourself you maimed, your father fought,
    And mother strove to kill;

When terror spread, and neighbours ran,
    Your dangerous strength to bind,
And soon, a howling crazy man
    Your limbs were fast confined—

How then you strove and shrieked aloud,
    Your bones and sinews bared,
And fiendish on the gazing crowd,
    With burning eye balls, glared—

And begged, and swore, and wept and prayed,
    With maniac laugh joined—
How fearful were those signs displayed
    By pangs that killed thy mind!

And when at length, the drear and long,
    Time soothed thy fiercer woes,
How plaintively thy mournful song
    Upon the stilly night rose—

I've heard it oft, as if I dreamed,
    Far distant, sweet, and lone—
The funeral dirge, it ever seemed
    Of reason dead and gone—

Poor Matthew! I have ne'er forgot,
    When first, with maddened will,
Yourself you maimed, your father fought,
    And mother strove to kill;

When terror spread, and neighbours ran,
    Your dange'rous strength to bind;
And soon, a howling crazy man
    Your limbs were fast confined.

How then you strove and shrieked aloud,
    Your bones and sinews bared;
And fiendish on the gazing crowd,
    With burning eye balls glared.

And begged, and swore, and wept and prayed,
    With maniac laugh joined.
How fearful were those signs displayed
    By pangs that killed thy mind!

And when at length, tho' drear and long,
    Time soothed thy fiercer woes,
How plaintively thy mournful song
    Upon the still night rose.

I've heard it oft, as if I dreamed,
    Far distant, sweet, and lone.
The funeral dirge, it ever seemed
    Of reason dead and gone.

What can it mean that Lincoln recalls of that beautiful, haunting dirge that he often "stole away" to hear it, "All stealthily and still"? The lines describing Lincoln's furtive pleasure in broken Matthew's song emerge into a mysterious simplicity concentrated like that of William Blake:

> Air held his breath; trees, with the spell,
>   Seemed sorrowing angels round,
> Whose swelling tears in dew-drops fell
>   Upon the listening ground.

Here a great prose writer attains actual poetry: an art between speech and music, evoked by Lincoln's term "canto." The lines reflect Lincoln's characteristic attainment of light and darkness on a monumental scale: his mind's clarity and mystery represented here in fellow-feeling and terror, the eerie mingling of magnetism and dread, eloquence and silence. ◄

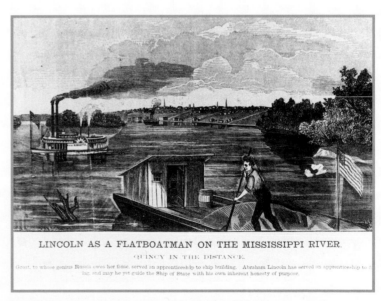

LINCOLN AS A FLATBOATMAN ON THE MISSISSIPPI RIVER.
QUINCY IN THE DISTANCE.
Great, to whose genius Russia owes her fame, served an apprenticeship to ship building. Abraham Lincoln has served an apprenticeship to the bar, and may he yet guide the Ship of State with his own inherent honesty of purpose.

Though Lincoln harbored no romantic illusions about his hardscrabble years in "the state of my early life," artists imagined highlights from his early pursuits—like piloting a flatboat—to promote the politician as an exemplar of American opportunity.

To drink its streams, I've stole away,
  All stealthily and still,
Ere yet the rising god of day
  Had streaked the eastern hill—

Air held his breath; trees, with the spell,
  Seemed sorrowing angels round,
Whose swelling tears in dew-drops fell
  Upon the listening ground—

But this is past; and nought remains,
  That raised thee o'er the brute.
Thy piercing shrieks, and soothing strains,
  Are like, forever mute—

Now fare thee well— More thou the cause,
  Than subject now of woe—
All mental pangs, by time's kind laws,
  Hast lost the power to know—

O death! Thou awe-inspiring prince,
  That keepst the world in fear;
Why dost thou tear more blest ones hence,
  And leave him ling'ring here?—

If I should ever send another, the subject will be a
"Bear hunt"—
                                Yours as ever.
                                    A. Lincoln

To drink its strains, I've stole away,
　　All stealthily and still,
Ere yet the rising god of day
　　Had streaked the Eastern hill.

Air held his breath; trees, with the spell,
　　Seemed sorrowing angels round,
Whose swelling tears in dew-drops fell
　　Upon the listening ground.

But this is past; and nought remains,
　　That raised thee o'er the brute.
Thy piercing shrieks, and soothing strains,
　　Are like, forever mute.

Now fare thee well — more thou the <u>cause</u>,
　　Than <u>subject</u> now of woe.
All mental pangs, by time's kind laws,
　　Hast lost the power to know.

O death! Thou awe-inspiring prince,
　　That keepst the world in fear;
Why dost thou tear more blest ones hence,
　　And leave him ling'ring here?
If I should ever send another, the subject will be a
"Bear hunt".　　　　　　　　　Yours as ever

　　　　　　　　　　　　　　　A. Lincoln

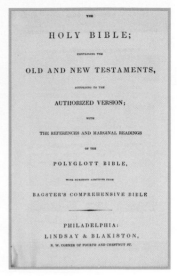

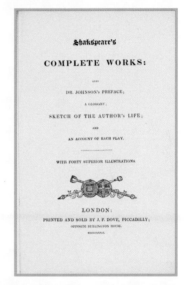

Lacking formal education, young Lincoln read voraciously, and particularly loved poetry. Three of the texts he surely read were the Bible and works by Shakespeare and Robert Burns. "Burns never touched a sentiment," he later told his secretary, "without carrying it to its ultimate expression, and leaving nothing further to be said."

LETTER TO **MARY LINCOLN**, APRIL 16, 1848

Mary Lincoln accompanied her husband to Washington for his 1847–48 term in the U.S. House of Representatives. But she soon returned—with their two boys, Robert and Edward—to live with her family in Lexington, Kentucky, where Lincoln wrote her.

Washington, April. 16- 1848-

Dear Mary:

In this troublesome world, we are never quite satisfied- When you were here, I thought you hindered me some in attending to business; but now, having nothing but business— no variety- it has grown exceedingly tasteless to me- I hate to sit down and direct documents, and I hate to stay in this old room by myself- You know I told you in last sunday's letter, I was going to make a little speech during the week; but the week has passed away without my getting a chance to do so; and now my interest in the subject has passed away too- Your second and third letters have been received since I wrote before. Dear Eddy thinks father is "gone tapila" Has any further discovery been made as to the breaking into your grand-mother's house?- If I were she, I would not remain there alone- You mention that your uncle John Parker is likely to be at Lexington- Dont forget to present him my very kindest regards—

I went yesterday to hunt the little plaid stockings, as you wished; but found that McKnight has quit business, and Allen has not a single pair of the description you give, and only one plain pair of any sort that I thought would fit "Eddy's dear little feet"- I have a notion to

Washington, April 16. 1848

Dear Mary:

In this troublesome world, we are never quite satisfied. When you were here, I thought you hindered me some in attending to business; but now, having nothing but business — no variety — it has grown exceedingly tasteless to me. I hate to sit down and direct documents and I hate to stay in this old room by myself. You know I told you in last sunday's letter, I was going to make a little speech during the week; but the week has passed away without my getting a chance to do so; and now my interest in the subject has passed away too. Your second and third letters have been received since I wrote before. Dear Eddy [thinks] thinks father is "<u>gone tapila</u>." Has any further discovery been made as to the breaking into your grand-mother's house? If I were she, I would not remain there alone. You mention that your uncle John Parker is likely to be at Lexington. Dont forget to present him my very kindest regards.

I went yesterday to hunt the little plaid stockings, as you wished; but found that McKnight has quit business, and Allen had not a single pair of the description you give, and only one [???] plaid pair of any sort that I thought would fit "Eddy's dear little feet". I have a notion to

JENNIFER FLEISCHNER

"In this troublesome world, we are never quite satisfied." It sounds like the beginning of a realist novel, an ironic comment upon the human condition. Yet, for Lincoln, this slightly distancing move, measured and balanced, allows him to reveal a deep personal need, as if to say, *I did not want you to stay, but now that you're gone I feel aimless and alone.* Even more: *Without you nothing is going right. The speech I wanted to make did not happen, and now I've lost interest in it. I could not even find the "little plaid stockings" you wanted me to buy.* The letter opens in this pensive, subdued mood, with its narrative of failure and mistake. Yet the very activity of writing seems to cheer Lincoln—to lift his depression—as he feels his way back through sentences and paragraphs into the intimacy of marriage.

By the middle of the letter he's found his footing, and gently chides Mary for this and that, teasing her about her weight and the trail of enemies she's left behind in their boardinghouse (revealing, perhaps, one of the difficulties Mary's presence in Washington created for him). Yet Lincoln cannot shake off the brooding anxiety that separation and loss will always engender in him. *The boys—don't let them forget me,* he pleads. ◄

make another trial to-morrow morning— If I could
get them, I have an excellent chance of sending
them— Mr Warrick Tunstall, of St Louis is here—
He is to leave early this week, and to go by Lexington—
He says he knows you, and will call to see you; and
he voluntarily asked, if I had not some package
to send to you—

I wish you to enjoy yourself in every possible way;
but is there no danger of wounding the feelings of
your good father, by being so openly intimate with
the Wickliffe family?

Mrs Broome has not removed yet; but she thinks
of doing so to-morrow— All the house— or rather, all
with whom you were on decided good terms— send
their love to you— The others say nothing—

Very soon after you went away, I got what I think
a very pretty set of shirt bosom studs— modest little
ones, jet set in gold, only costing 50 cents a piece, or 1.50
for the whole—

Suppose you do not prefer the "Hon" to the address on your letters to me any more— I like the letters
very much, but I would rather they should not
have that upon them— It is not necessary, as I suppose
you have thought, to have them to come free—

And you are entirely free from headache? That is good

make another trial tomorrow morning. If I could

get them, I have an excellent chance of sending

them. Mr. Warrick Tunstall, of St. Louis is here.

He is to leave early this week, and to go by Lexington.

He says he knows you, and will call to see you; and

he voluntarily asked, if I had not some package

to send to you.

I wish you to enjoy yourself in every possible way;

but is there no danger of wounding the feelings of

your good father, by being so openly intimate with

the Wickliffe family?

Mrs. Broome has not removed yet; but she thinks

of doing so tomorrow. All the house — or rather, all

with whom you were on decided good terms — send

their love to you. The others say nothing.

Very soon after you went away, I got what I think

a very pretty set of shirt-bosom studs — modest little

ones, jet set in gold, only costing 50 cents a piece, or 1.50

for the whole.

Suppose you do not prefix the "Hon" to the ad-

dress on your letters to me any more. I like the letters

very much, but I would rather they should not

have that upon them. It is not necessary, as I suppose

you have thought, to have them to come free.

And you are entirely free from head-ache? That is good

The earliest known photograph of Mary Lincoln, ca.
1846. A bewitching belle in her youth, she could, a
contemporary testified, "make a bishop forget
his vows."

— good — considering it is the first spring you have been free from it since we were acquainted — I am afraid you will get so well, and fat, and young, as to be wanting to marry again — Tell Louisa I want her to watch you a little for me — Get weighed and write me how much you weigh —

I did not get rid of the impression of that foolish dream about dear Bobby, till I got your letter written the same day — What did he and Eddy think of the little letters father sent them? Dont let the blessed fellows forget father —

A day or two ago Mr. Strong, here in Congress, said to me that Matilda would visit here within two or three weeks — Suppose you write her a letter, and enclose it in one of mine; and if she comes I will deliver it to her, and if she does not, I will send it to her —

Most affectionately
A. Lincoln

— good — considering it is the first spring you have been free

from it since we were acquainted. I am afraid you will

get so well, and fat, and young, as to be wanting to marry

again. Tell Louisa I want her to watch you a little

for me. Get weighed, and write me how much you weigh.

I did not get rid of the impression of that foolish

dream about dear Bobby till I got your letter written

the same day. What did he and Eddy think of the

little letters father sent them? Dont let the blessed fel-

lows forget father.

A day or two ago Mr. Strong, here in Congress,

said to me that Matilda would visit here within two

or three weeks. Suppose you write her a letter, and

enclose it in one of mine; and if she comes I will

deliver it to her, and if she does not, I will send

it to her.   Most affectionately

A. Lincoln

The original Bullfinch dome still towered above it—
and its now-familiar east and west wings had yet to
appear—when John Plumbe took the first photograph
ever made of the United States Capitol.

His political career on the skids after an unpopular stand against the Mexican–American War, Lincoln seems to have been considering a career on the lyceum circuit. This unfinished sketch on the mighty Niagara may have been intended as a draft for a public lecture.

Niagara-Falls! By what mysterious power is it, that millions and millions, are drawn from all parts of the world, to gaze upon Niagara Falls? There is no mystery about the thing itself. Every effect is just such as any intelligent man, knowing the causes, would anticipate, without it. If the water moving onward in a great river, reaches a point where there is a perpendicular jog, of a hundred feet in descent, in the bottom of the river, it is plain the water will have a violent and continuous pilings at that point. It is also plain the water, thus plunging, will foam, and roar, and send up a mist, continuously, in which last, during sunshine, there will be perpetual rain-bows. The mere physical of Niagara Falls, is only this. Yet this is really a very small part of that world's wonder. It's power to excite reflection, and emotion, is its great charm. The geologist will demonstrate that the plunge, or fall, was once at Lake Ontario, and has worn its way back to it's present position; he will ascertain how fast it is wearing now, and so get a basis for determining how long it has been wearing back from Lake Ontario, and finally demonstrate by it that this world is at least fourteen thousand years old. A philosopher of a slightly different turn will say Niagara Falls is only the lip of the basin out of which pours all the surplus water which rains down on two or three hundred thousand square miles of the earth's surface. He will estimate with approximate accuracy, that five hundred thousand thousand [tons] of water, falls with it's full weight, a distance of a hundred feet each minute- thus exerting a force equal to the lifting of the same weight, through the same space, in the same time. And then the further reflection comes that this vast amount of water, constantly pouring down, is supplied by an equal amount constantly lifted up, by the sun; and still he says, "If this...

Niagara Falls! By what mysterious power is it, that millions and millions, are drawn from all parts of the world, to gaze upon Niagara Falls? There is no mystery about the thing itself. Every effect is just such as any inteligent ^man knowing the causes, would anticipate, without it. If the water moving onward in a great river, reac[hes] a point when there is a perpendicular jog, of a hundred feet in descent, in the bottom of the river, it is plain the water will have a violent and continuous plunge at that point. It is also plain the water, thus plunging, will foam, and roar, and send up a mist, continuously, in which last, during sunshine, there will be perpetual rain-bows. The mere physical of Niagara Falls, is only this. Yet this is really a very small part of that world's wonder. It's power to excite reflection, and emotion, is it's great charm. The geologist will demonstrate that the plunge or fall, was once at Lake Ontario, and has worn it's way back to it's present position; he will ascertain how <u>fast</u> it is wearing now, and so get a basis for determining how <u>long</u> it has been wearing back from Lake Ontario, and finally demonstrate ^by it that the world is at least fourteen thousand years old. A philosopher of a slightly different turn will say Niagara Falls is only the lip of the basin out of which pours all the surplus water which rains down on two or three hundred thousand square miles of the earths surface. He will estimate w[ith] approximate accuracy, that five hundred thousand [to]ns of water, falls with it's full weight, a distance of a hundred feet each minute — thus exerting a force equal to the lifting of the same weight, through the same space, in the same time. And then the further reflection comes that this vast amount of water, constantly pouring <u>down</u>, is supplied by an equal amount constantly <u>lifted up</u>, by the sun; and still he says, "If this

CYNTHIA OZICK

Lincoln knew rivers, and to know rivers was to be intimate with currents and channels, headwaters and feeders, lakes and falls and spectrumed mists. In 1828, at nineteen, he joined the crew of a flatboat carrying goods to New Orleans. By twenty-one he was a seasoned and canny riverman; so it should not surprise that he was drawn to reflect on Niagara's bellowing forces. What genuinely startles is the *science,* the drive to encompass the physical knowledge that will explain nature empirically, through dispassionate geological understanding. For Lincoln, Niagara Falls is an experiment in a terrestrial laboratory designed to produce a proof: the age of the earth.

"The geologist," he writes, "will demonstrate that the plunge, or fall, was once at Lake Ontario, and has worn its way back to its present position; he will ascertain how fast it is wearing now, and so get a basis for determining . . . that this world is at least fourteen thousand years old." This observation was set down in the late 1840s; astrophysics was unforeseen. Here it is not Lincoln who falters, but the limited science of his era. And still his exposition of the formation of the falls cannot be challenged.

(continued)

41

which is lifted up, for this one space of two or three
hundred thousand square miles, an equal amount
must be lifted for every other equal space; and
he is overwhelmed in the contemplation of the
vast power the sun is constantly exerting in
quiet, noiseless opperation of lifting water up to
[be rained] down again—
But still there is more. It calls up the indefinite
past— When Columbus first sought this continent—
when Christ suffered on the cross— when Moses led
Israel through the Red-Sea— nay, even, when Adam
first came from the hand of his Maker— then
as now, Niagara was roaring
here— The eyes of that species of extinct giants, whose
bones fill the Mounds of America, have gazed on
Niagara, as ours do now— Cotemporary with the
whole race of men, and older than the first
man, Niagara is strong, and fresh to-day as ten thousand
years ago— The Mammoth and Mastadon— now
so long dead, that fragments of their monstrous bones,
alone testify, that they ever lived, have gazed
on Niagara— In that long—long time, never still
for a single moment— Never dried, never
froze, never slept, never rested,

42

much is lifted up, for <u>this one</u> space of two or three hundred thousand square miles, an equal amount must be lifted for every other equal space; an[d] he is overwhelmed in the contemplation of t[he] vast power the sun is constantly exerting in [the] quiet, noisless opperation of lifting water <u>up</u> t[o be] rained <u>down</u> again.

But still there is more. It calls up the indefinite past. When Columbus first sought this continent — when Christ suffered on the Cross — when Moses led Israel through the ~~red~~ Red-Sea — nay, even, when Ad- first came from the hand of his Maker — am ~~was made~~ then as now, Niagara was roaring here. The eyes of that species of extinct giants, whose bones fill the Mounds of America, have gazed on Niagara, as ours do now. Cotemporary with the whole race of ~~man,~~ ^{men,} and older than the first man, Niagara is ^{strong and} ∧ fresh to-day as ten thousand years ago. The Mammoth and Mastodon now so long dead, that fragments of their monstrous bones, alone testify, that they ever lived, have gazed on Niagara. In that long — long time, never still for a single moment — Never dried, never froze, never slept, never rested,

Lincoln and science! A juxtaposition we must now weave into our national portrait, perhaps too marmoreally statuesque, as Niagara itself is too often fixed into a kind of gigantically heroic sculpture. How unmythical, how *factual,* is Lincoln's Niagara, "the lip of the basin out of which pours all the surplus water which rains down on two or three hundred square miles of the earth's surface."

But here lives the other Lincoln too, the poet of the Gettysburg Address, in equal step with the geologist: the metaphysical Lincoln who drills through the old bones of time, for whom ceaseless Niagara is both measured tonnage and the immeasurable weight of millennia. "Never dried, never froze, never slept, never rested," he sings. Eight extraordinary English words, yet each one commonplace and clear as a drop of water.

Of which lasting hymns are made. ◀

Congressman Lincoln took an indirect route home from Washington—charging taxpayers for the costly detour—just to visit Niagara Falls. His first reaction was prosaic, wondering "where in the world did all the water come from," but the falls soon moved him to lyricism.

Lincoln's advice to aspiring attorneys—likely drafted to fit into a lecture he never finished or delivered—nicely embodies the diligence, moral rectitude, and common sense he exuded in his thirties and forties. *(Excerpt)*

I am not an accomplished lawyer. I find quite as much material for a lecture, in those points wherein I have failed, as in those wherein I have been moderately successful.

The leading rule for the lawyer, as for the man of every other calling, is diligence. Leave nothing for to-morrow, which can be done to-day. Never let your correspondence fall behind. Whatever piece of business you have in hand, before stopping, do all the labor pertaining to it, which can then be done. When you bring a common-law suit, if you have the facts for doing so, write the declaration at once. If a law point be involved, examine the books, and note the authority you rely on, upon the declaration itself, where you are sure to find it when wanted. The same of defences and pleas. In business not likely to be litigated,—ordinary collection cases, foreclosures, partitions, and the like,—make all examinations of titles, and note them, and even draft orders and decrees in advance. This course has a triple ad-

vantage; it avoids omissions and neglect, saves your labor, when once done; performs the labor out of court when you have leisure, rather than in court, when you have not.

Extemporaneous speaking should be practiced and cultivated. It is the lawyer's avenue to the public. However able and faithful he may be in other respects, people are slow to bring him business, if he can not make a speech. And yet there is not a more fatal error to young lawyers, than relying too much on speech-making. If any one, upon his rare powers of speaking, shall claim an exemption from the drudgery of the law, his case is a failure in advance.

Discourage litigation. Persuade your neighbors to compromise whenever you can. Point out to them how the nominal winner is often a real loser, in fees, expenses, and waste of time. As a peace-maker, the lawyer has a superior opportunity of being a good man. There will still be business enough.

I am not an accomplished lawyer. I find quite as much material for a lecture in those points wherein I have failed, as in those
wherein I have been moderately successful.

The leading rule for the lawyer, as for the man of every other calling,
is <u>diligence</u>. Leave nothing for to-morrow, which can be done to-day.
Never let your correspondence fall behind. Whatever piece of business you have in hand, before stopping, do all the labor pertaining to it which can <u>then</u> be done. When you bring a common-law suit, if you have the facts for doing so, write the declaration at once. If a law point be involved, examine the books,
and note the authority you rely on, upon the declaration
itself, where you are sure to find it when wanted. The same
of defences and pleas. In business not likely to be litigated — ordinary collection cases, foreclosures, partitions, and the
                                  and note them,
like — make all examinations of titles ∧ and even draft orders
and decrees in advance. This course has a triple ad-

vantage; it avoids omissions and neglect, <u>saves</u> your labor when
once done, performs the labor out of court when you <u>have</u>
leisure, rather than in court, when you have not.

Extemporaneous speaking should be practiced and cultivated.
It is the lawyer's avenue to the public. However able
and faithful he may be in other respects, people are
slow to bring him business if he cannot make a
speech. And yet there is not a more fatal error
to young lawyers, than relying too much on speech-making. If any one, upon his rare powers of speaking, shall claim an
exemption from the drudgery of the law, his case is a failure
in advance.
      Discourage
~~Never encourage~~ litigation. Persuade your neighbors to compromise whenever you can. Point out to them how the <u>nomin-</u>
<u>al</u> winner is often a <u>real</u> loser, in fees, expenses, and
waste of time. As a peacemaker the lawyer has a superior opertunity of being a good man. There will still
be business enough.

𝒮ANDRA DAY O'CONNOR

Abraham Lincoln was a lawyer in
Illinois before becoming president of
the United States. His practice was
that of a local lawyer with a wide
variety of cases. His notes for advice
to lawyers are as timely and wise
today as when he wrote them in the
1850s. For example, his first piece of
advice is to be "diligent" in
preparation, even if the work is
tedious. His second bit of advice to
the lawyer is to "discourage
litigation," to try to be a peacemaker
rather than one who stirs up
litigation. Third, Mr. Lincoln wrote
that "an exorbitant fee should never
be claimed." Finally, and most
important, he advised that every
lawyer must "resolve to be honest." If
"you cannot be an honest lawyer,
resolve to be honest without being a
lawyer."

Lincoln's advice can and should
guide all lawyers today as well as
those who aspire to practice law.
There is no better way to honor this
great man. ◄

Lincoln's earliest law office was a meagerly furnished
room above the county courtroom in "Hoffman's Row,"
a new Springfield office building. Here a later legal
office is draped in black in his memory.

45

Scholars remain uncertain as to why—or even precisely when—Lincoln composed this enduringly simple definition of the necessary role of government, but its author surely never suspected that politicians would be guided by it for generations to come.

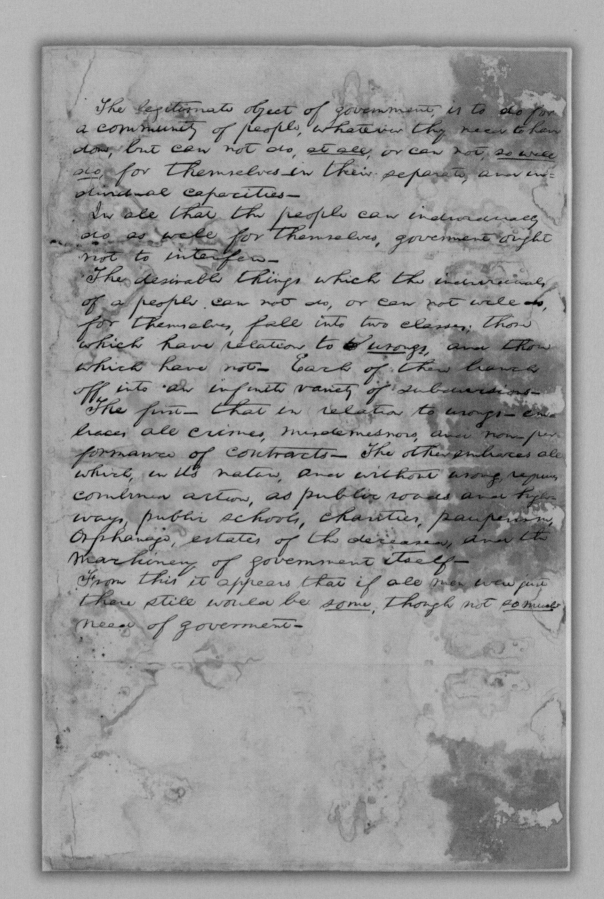

The legitimate object of government, is to do for a community of people, whatever they need to have done, but can not do, <u>at all</u>, or can not, <u>so well do</u>, for themselves — in their separate, and individual capacities.

In all that the people can individually do as well for themselves, government ought not to interfere.

The desirable things which the individuals of a people can not do, or can not well do, for themselves, fall into two classes; those which have relation to ~~to~~ <u>wrongs</u>, and those which have not. Each of these branch off into an infinite variety of subdivisions.

The first — that in relation to wrongs — embraces all crimes, misdemeanors, and non-performance of contracts. The other embraces all which, in its nature, and without wrong, requires combined action, as public roads and highways, public schools, charities, pauperism, orphanages, estates of the deceased, and the machinery of government itself.

From this it appears that if all men were just there still would be <u>some</u>, though not <u>so much</u>, need of government.

$\mathcal{M}$ARIO M. CUOMO

Some of the most rancorous and least useful political debates revolve around the question of what precise role the government should play beyond the most obvious: to protect us from enemies who seek to injure or destroy the nation. Thus, those who call themselves conservatives are inclined to disparage government in general and "big" government in particular. That simplistic view ignores the best argument for the use of government, which is to advance the whole society's well-being.

Perhaps Lincoln's most valuable contribution to the debate was providing a cogent, plain-English formula for determining what specific functions government should undertake. Around 1854 he honed his credo and described the role of government with sparkling simplicity, comprehensiveness, and intelligence.

Lincoln could express himself in words that approached poetry. But even in basic prose, no one ever offered a more timeless argument for why Americans need a government that works. ◄

Lincoln proudly holds the pro-Republican *Chicago Tribune*—a staunch ally in the Republican struggle to redefine government—for this 1854 portrait by Chicago photographer Polycarpus von Schneidau.

Ambrotype by T. B. Pearson, Macomb, Illinois, August 26, 1858

Part Two

"A HOUSE DIVIDED AGAINST ITSELF"

1854-1861

In the early 1850s, after a disappointing term in Congress had dimmed his prospects, Lincoln was practically retired from politics. But in 1854, the repeal of the Missouri Compromise—which threatened to allow slavery into a vast swath of Western territory—roused him to action. To a remarkable degree, his most vital action was literary. Lincoln ran twice for the United States Senate, and helped to build the new Republican party in Illinois. But he really made history in the late 1850s by exposing in speeches and letters the fissure that slavery caused in American life—and the mortal threat that slavery expansion posed to the Union and its original promise of equality. In private notes and fragments—on the Dred Scott decision, for example—he worked out perfect phrasing and ground complex ideas down to their nubs, so that by the time he mounted the stage, audiences were dazzled. And when his speeches circulated among friendly newspapers, his reputation spread beyond Illinois.

Despite his impressive rise, few beyond his most ardent partisans—one of whom solicited from him his first autobiographical sketch—considered the fifty-year-old Lincoln presidential material in late 1859. When, to much surprise, he landed the Republican nomination—by satisfying divergent wings of the party while offending no one—he had to introduce himself to the divided nation. And after his election, he bid farewell to his home knowing that he faced a task "greater than that which rested upon Washington." The first president had inaugurated a nation. Lincoln, with his deeds—and, especially, his words—would have to hold it together.

FRAGMENT ON DRED SCOTT DECISION, CA. DECEMBER 1856

The Supreme Court's Dred Scott decision of March 6, 1857—authorizing the nationalizing of slavery and ruling that blacks could never be American citizens—dominated much of Lincoln's oratory for the next several years. As this early fragment indicates—it was written at the end of 1856 or, at latest, January 1857—he was developing arguments in opposition even before the Court rendered its decision.

What would be the effect of this, if it should ever be the creed of a dominant party in the nation? Let us analyse, and consider it—

It affirms that, whatever decision the Supreme Court may decide as to the Constitutional restriction on the power of a territorial Legislature, in regard to slavery in the territory, must be obeyed, and enforced by all the departments of the federal government—

Now, if this is sound, as to this particular Constitutional question, it is equally sound of all constitutional questions; so that the proposition substantially, is "Whatever decision the Supreme Court makes on any constitutional question, must be obeyed, and enforced by all the departments of the federal government"—

Again, it is not the full scope of this creed, that if the Supreme Court, having the particular question before them, shall decide that Dred Scott is a slave, the executive department must enforce the decision against Dred Scott— If this were its full scope, it is presumed, no one would controvert its' correctness— But in this narrow scope, there is no room for the Legislative department to enforce the decision; while the creed affirms that all the departments must en-force it— The creed, then, has a broader scope; and what is it? It is this; that

so soon as the Supreme Court decides that Dred Scott is a slave, the whole community must decide that not only Dred Scott, but that all persons in like condition, are rightfully slaves

What would be the effect of this, if it should ever
be the creed of a dominant party in the nation?
Let us analyse, and consider it.

that whatever

It affirms ~~thatever decision~~ the Supreme Court
may decide as to the Constitutional restrictions on
the power of a teritorial Legislature, in regard to
slavery in the teritory, must be obeyed, and enforced by all the departments of the federal
government.

constitutional

Now, if this is sound, as to this particular ^ question, it is equally sound of all constitutional questions; so that the proposition substantially is
"Whatever decision the Supreme Court makes on
any constitutional question, must be obeyed,
and enforced by all the departments of the
federal government."

Again, it is not the full scope of this creed,
that if the Supreme Court, having the particular
question before them, shall decide that Dred
Scott is a slave, the executive department must
enforce the decision against Dred Scott. If this
were it's full scope, it is presumed, no one would
controvert its correctness. But in this narrow
scope, there is no room for the Legislative department to enforce the decision; while the creed
affirms that all the departments must enforce it. The creed, then, has a broader
scope; and what is it? It is this; that

so soon as the Supreme Court decides that
Dred Scott is a slave, the whole community
must decide that not only Dred Scott,
but that all persons in like condition, are
rightfully
slaves

ⱲALTER MOSLEY

Many creative writers have long held that
politics and prose do not intersect. They
believe that a pure writer's political beliefs
have no place in his or her fiction. This belief
has long served to leech the life's blood out of
much of American fiction and to marginalize
some of our potentially greatest writers.

This footnote to modern education is
brought to mind when I am faced with the
extraordinary prose of our sixteenth president.
Abraham Lincoln was, of course, not a
novelist. He wrote speeches that moved a
nation past its inner contradictions toward an
ideal state (a state that we have yet to attain).
He stirred the democratic spirit and shook the
moral underpinnings of Americans by speaking
to them in simple and irrefutable terms that
changed the direction of our polity. In his
work, which often began with notes and
fragments, such as this piece on the Dred
Scott decision, he literally re-created a nation
out of words: the greatest achievement that
any writer can hope for.

As I have said, Mr. Lincoln's speeches were
not novels. They weren't fiction but they were
stories still and all. He created, in his
speechifying, a possible world that was both
potential and dream. He made a world out of
Americans' imaginations and created the
possibility for change.

As a novelist and storyteller in this world
today, I am more affected by this towering
historical figure of true literature than by all
the classes and strictures of myriad creative
writing teachers. Abraham Lincoln teaches us
that truth can be held in language and that
that truth, properly maintained and cared for,
can make the mighty out of the meek and the
righteous out of a reprobate nation.

What better, what more important story is
there to be told? ◄

ON STEPHEN DOUGLAS, CA. DECEMBER 1856

Even as Lincoln's star rose in the 1850s, he kept losing elections
while his nemesis Senator Stephen Douglas achieved greater power and glory.
In this private note, he cuts to the heart of the rivalry and, in so doing,
articulates his real life's purpose.

Twentytwo years ago judge Douglas and
I first became acquainted— We were both
young then; he, a trifle younger than I.
Even then, we were both ambitious; I,
perhaps, quite as much so as he— With
me, the race of ambition has been a
failure— a flat failure; with him it has
been one of splendid success— His name
fills the nation; and is not unknown, even, in
foreign lands— I affect no contempt
for the high eminence he has reached—
So reached, that the oppressed of my
species, might have shared with me
in the elevation, I would rather stand
on that eminence, then wear the richest
crown that ever pressed a monarch's brow—

MICHAEL BURLINGAME

Twentytwo years ago Judge Douglas and I first became acquainted. We were both young then; he a trifle younger than I. Even then, we were both ambitious; I, perhaps, quite as much so as he. With me, the race of ambition has been a failure — a flat failure; with him it has been one of splendid success. His name fills the nation; and [????????], even, [??] in foreign lands. I affect no contempt for the high eminence he has reached. So reached, that the oppressed of my species, might have shared with me in the elevation, I would rather stand on that eminence, than wear the richest crown that ever pressed a monarch's brow.

It is difficult to imagine that a man so widely revered as Lincoln could have suffered from an inferiority complex, but these poignant words clearly indicate that he did before he became famous. He was embarrassed by what he called his "deficient" education, by his homeliness, by the poverty in which he grew up, by his shiftless father, by his mother's promiscuous family, by his lack of social polish, as well as by his relative obscurity (especially compared to Douglas, with whom he had been competing for nearly two decades). His sense of failure propelled him into a midlife crisis in his early forties, during which he somehow transformed himself from a party hack into a true statesman.

Remarkably, he remained humble even after his great success. Shortly before he died, he told a friend: "I am very sure that if I do not go away from here a wiser man, I shall go away a better man, for having learned here what a very poor sort of a man I am." This private memo, like others that have survived, affords more insight into Lincoln's thoughts than do his formal letters and speeches. ◄

Lincoln decried Stephen Douglas's characteristic "assumption of superiority," but conceded the Little Giant knew "just how to appeal to…prejudices and was a very powerful opponent, both on and off the stump."

Stephen Douglas was far more famous than Lincoln through much of their long political rivalry, and his Vermont birthplace emerged as a landmark long before Lincoln's log cabin achieved preeminence.

"I am naturally anti-slavery," Lincoln would write as president. "I can not remember when I did not so think, and feel." This persuasive rumination on the dominant issue of his political life testified to his long-standing, freedom-loving instincts, poignantly expressed in the year of his debates with Douglas.

I have never professed an indifference to the honors of official station; and were I to do so now, I should only make myself ridiculous. Yet I have never failed— do not now fail— to remember that in the republican cause there is a higher aim than that of mere office— I have not allowed myself to forget that the abolition of the Slave-trade by Great Brittain, was agitated a hundred years before it was a final success; that the measure had its open fire-eating opponents; its stealthy "dont care" opponents; its dollar and cent opponents; its inferior race opponents; its negro equality opponents; and its religion and good order opponents; that all these opponents got offices, and their adversaries got none— But I have also remembered that, though, they blazed, like tallow-candles for a century, at last they flickered in the socket, died out, stank in the dark for a brief season, and were remembered no more, even by the smell— School-boys know that Wilberforce, and Granville Sharpe, helped that cause forward; but who can now name a single man who labored to retard it? Remembering these things I can not but regard it as possible that the higher object of this contest may not be completely, attained within

the term of my, natural life. But I can not doubt either that it will come in due time. Even in this view, I am proud, in my passing speck of time, to contribute an humble mite to that glorious consummation, which my own poor eyes may not last to see—

I have never professed an indifference to the
honors of official station; and were I to do so
now, I should only make myself ridiculous.
Yet I have never failed — do not now fail —
to remember that in the republican cause
there is a higher aim than that of mere office. I have not allowed myself to forget
that the abolition of the Slave-trade by
Great Brittain, was agitated a hundred
years before it was a final success; that
the measure had it's open fire-eating opponents; it's stealthy "dont care" opponents;
it's dollar and cent opponents; it's inferior
race opponents; its negro equality opponents;
and its religion and good order opponents; that all these opponents got offices,
and their adversaries got none. But I
have also remembered that ^ though they blazed,
like tallow-candles for a century, at last
they flickered in the socket, died out,
stank in the dark for a brief season,
and were remembered no more, even by
the smell. School-boys know that
Wilbeforce, and Granville Sharpe, helped
that cause forward; but who can now
name a single man who labored
to retard it? Remembering these things
I can not but regard it as possible
that the higher object of this contest
may not be completely attained within

the term of my ^ natural life. But I can not
doubt either that it will come in due
time. Even in this view, I am proud, in my
passing speck of time, to contribute an
humble mite to that glorious consummation, which my own poor eyes may ~~never~~ not
last to see.

William Wilberforce could not be indifferent
to slavery. For twenty years, the wealthy heir to
a merchant fortune worked unceasingly to end
slavery in the British Empire. His labor bore
fruit when Parliament acted in 1807 to abolish
the slave trade.

Abraham Lincoln admired the Herculean
efforts exerted by Wilberforce. Like his
English counterpart, Lincoln could not be
indifferent to the immorality of slavery.
Lincoln and Wilberforce embraced the natural
law principle of the equality of all men.
Wilberforce drew upon the words of St. Paul:
"God hath made of one blood all nations of
men." Lincoln found his text in the "self-
evident" equality principle of the Declaration
of Independence: "All men are created equal."

In this speech fragment, Lincoln joins
high principle to an honorable ambition,
observing that "in the republican cause there is
a higher aim than that of mere office." The
self-tutored lawyer from Illinois could not
understand those "dont care" politicians, such
as Senator Stephen A. Douglas, who pretended
indifference to involuntary servitude. Such
men reminded Lincoln of Wilberforce's
opponents who "blazed," "flickered," and
"died," whereas the memory of Wilberforce
endured.

Well-remembered for his first major,
printed, antislavery speech of 1854 at Peoria,
Lincoln would thereafter campaign tirelessly
against the spread of slavery. He often
predicted—as he does here—that slavery
might not be extinguished in the United
States "within the term of my natural life."
On January 31, 1865—only a few months
before his assassination—Congress passed the
Thirteenth Amendment to abolish slavery.
Lincoln himself had contributed more than his
"humble mite to that glorious
consummation." ◄

DRAFT OF THE "HOUSE DIVIDED" ADDRESS, JUNE 1858

As early as 1855 Lincoln privately confided his worry that the nation could not "continue together…half slave, and half free." But not until the winter of 1857–1858 did he link this concern to the biblical warning: "a house divided against itself cannot stand." That June, the ideas at last evolved into one of his greatest speeches. But the "House Divided" manuscript vanished. This fragment is all that survives.

Why, Kansas is neither the _whole_, nor a _tithe_ of the real question—

"A house divided against itself can not stand."

I believe this government can not endure permanently, half slave, and half free—

I expressed this belief a year ago; and subsequent developements have but confirmed me.

I do not expect the Union to be dissolved—I do not expect the house to fall; but I _do_ expect it will cease to be divided—It will become _all_ one thing, or _all_ the other—Either the opponents of slavery will arrest the further spread of it, and put it in course of ultimate extinction; or its advocates will push it forward till it shall become alike lawful in _all_ the states, old, as well as new—Do you doubt it? Study the Dred Scott decision, and then see, how little, even now, remains to be done—

That decision may be reduced to three points—The first is, that a negro can not be a citizen—That point is made in order to deprive the negro in every possible event, of the benefit of that provision of the U. S. Constitution which declares that;

"The _citizens_ of each State shall be entitled to all privileges and immunities of citizens in the several States"

The second point is, that the U. S. constitution protects slavery, as property, in all the U. S. territories, and that neither congress, nor the people of the territories, nor any other power, can prohibit it, at any time prior to the formation of State constitutions—

This point is made, in order that the territories may safely be filled up with slaves, before the formation of State constitutions, and thereby to embarass the free state

Why, Kansas is neither the <u>whole</u>, nor a
<u>tithe</u> of the real question.

"A house divided against itself can not
stand"

I believe this government can not endure
permanently, half slave, and half free.

I expressed this belief a year ago; and
subsequent developments have but confirmed me.

I do not expect the Union to be dissolved. I do not expect the house to fall; but
I <u>do</u> expect it will cease to be divided. It
will become <u>all</u> one thing, or <u>all</u> the other. Either
the opponents of slavery will arrest the further spread
of it, and put it in course of ultimate extinction; or
its advocates will push it forward till it shall become alike lawful in <u>all</u> the states, old, as well
as new. Do you doubt it? Study the Dred Scott
decision, and then see, how little, even now, remains
to be done.

That decision may be reduced to three points.
The first is, that a negro can not be a citizen.
That point is made in order to deprive the negro
in every possible event, of the benefit of that provision of the U.S Constitution which declares that:
"The <u>citizens</u> of each State shall be entitled to
all privileges and immunities of citizens in the
several States"

The second point is, that the U.S constitution protects slavery, as property, in all the U.S. territories, and
that neither Congress, nor the people of the territories,
nor any other power, can prohibit it, at any time pri-
or to the formation of State constitutions.

This point is made, in order that the territories may
safely be filled up with slaves, <u>before</u> the formation of
State constitutions, and thereby to embarrass the free states.

RICHARD J. DURBIN

The original challenge, from one old political
rival to another, was short and stunningly
understated. It made no mention of slavery or
even debates. Yet, Stephen Douglas worried to
a supporter, "I shall have my hands full."

Lincoln had already established himself as
his party's first and only choice for Senate
candidate—highly unusual in the 1850s—
when he challenged Douglas to a number of
"joint appearances" during their 1858 Senate
contest. He had been elevated to national
prominence by his extraordinary "House
Divided" speech, with its vivid prediction of
America's future and the coming war.
Fortunately for history, while Lincoln tossed
away the original manuscript of that prophetic
oration, he had begun drafting key phrases
months earlier, and later copied the sentiments
for admirers. Precious fragments of these
handwritten drafts and copies, such as the
excerpt here, remain.

The seven Lincoln-Douglas debates were,
at times, raucous political spectacles. But the
question at the heart of the debates was as
serious as any America has ever faced: Could a
nation dedicated to the principle that all men
are created equal forever deny liberty to some
of its people and still survive?

Lincoln's loss to Douglas turned out to
be, in his words, "a slip and not a fall." He
made sure the defeat would ultimately benefit
him by making a scrapbook copy of the debate
transcripts, editing them carefully, and seeing
to their publication.

Through the debates, Lincoln gained a
national prominence that would soon elevate
him to the presidency—and slavery took on a
moral urgency that would make a national
reckoning inevitable. ◄

The candidate biography was as crucial to the nineteenth-century campaign as television ads are to the twenty-first. Lincoln's friend Jesse Fell prevailed on him to provide this sketch, which Fell sent to a newspaperman in Pennsylvania. Notice, on the first page of the sketch, how Lincoln found the voice of the Indiana frontier when he revised "reading, writing, and Arithmetic" to "readin, writin, and cipherin."

Springfield, Dec. 20. 1859

J. W. Fell, Esq
    My dear Sir:

        Herewith is a little sketch, as you
requested— There is not much of it, for the reason,
I suppose, that there is not much of me—
If any thing be made out of it, I wish it
to be modest, and not to go beyond the materials—
If it was thought necessary to incorporate any thing
from any of my speeches, I suppose there would
be no objection— Of course it must not appear
to have been written by myself— Yours very truly
                                            A. Lincoln

Springfield, Dec. 20. 1859

J. W. Fell, Esq.

My dear Sir:

                Herewith is a little sketch, as you

requested. There is not much of it, for the reason,

I suppose, that there is not much of me.

    If anything be made out of it, I wish it

to be modest, and not to go beyond the materials.

If it were thought necessary to incorporate any thing

from any of my speeches, I suppose there would

be no objection. Of course it must not appear

to have been written by myself.   Yours very truly

                        A. Lincoln

KATHRYN HARRISON

For a twenty-first-century American reader, whose political default is cynicism, it seems almost subversive for a presidential nominee to present himself as Lincoln does in this sketch. What can it mean to be so guileless? Given an opportunity any politician would consider invaluable—to provide his own autobiography to journalists—Lincoln fails to exploit it. Or does he?

He offers a brief history of his forebears and his youth (including an account of his plain education in a place where "there was absolutely nothing to excite ambition for education" and where a Latin speaker would be looked upon "as a wizzard"), modestly summarizes his adventures and accomplishments, and ends on a witty and self-deprecating personal description. (The phrase "no other marks or brands recollected" was typically used to describe stray animals.) In the whole piece, the only reference to his fiery political career is the nonstatement that it's "pretty well known."

The feint is so nimble that it makes a reader wonder: Did the evolution of this extraordinary autodidact include his studying Cicero? Can Lincoln have been as pure a statesman as he seems? Or was he, rather, so consummate a politician as to appear purely a statesman? ◄

1

I was born Feb. 12. 1809, in Hardin County, Kentucky. My parents were both born in Virginia, of undistinguished families—second families, perhaps I should say. My mother, who died in my tenth year, was of a family of the name of Hanks, some of whom now reside in Adams, and others in Macon counties, Illinois— My paternal grandfather, Abraham Lincoln, emigrated from Rockingham County, Virginia, to Kentucky, about 1781 or 2, where, a year or two later, he was killed by indians, not in battle, but by stealth, when he was laboring to open a farm in the forest— His ancestors, who were quakers, went to Virginia from Berks County, Pennsylvania— An effort to identify them with the New England family of the same name ended in nothing more definite, than a similarity of Christian names in both families, such as Enoch, Levi, Mordecai, Solomon, Abraham, and the like—

My father, at the death of his father, was but six years of age; and he grew up, literally without education— He removed from Kentucky to what is now Spencer county, Indiana, in my eighth year— We reached our new home about the time the State came into the union— It was a wild region, with many bears and other wild animals, still in the woods— There I grew up— There were some schools, so called; but no qualification was ever required of a teacher, beyond "readin, writin, and cipherin", to the Rule of Three— If a straggler supposed to understand latin, happened to sojourn in

I was born Feb. 12, 1809, in Hardin County, Kentucky

My parents were both born in Virginia, of undistin-
       second families, perhaps I should say.
guished families — ^ My Mother, who died in my
tenth
~~ninth~~ year, was of a family of the name of Hanks,

some of whom now reside in Adams, and others

in Macon counties, Illinois. My paternal grand-

father, Abraham Lincoln, emigrated from Rock-

ingham County, Virginia, to Kentucky, about 1781 or

2, where, a year or two later, he was killed by

indians, not in battle, but by stealth, when he

was laboring to open a farm in the forest.

His ancestors, who were quakers, went to Virginia

from Berks County, Pennsylvania. An effort to
                  of the same name
identify them with the New-England family ^ end-

ed in nothing more definite, than a similarity

of Christian names in both families, such as

Enoch, Levi, Mordecai, Solomon, Abraham, and

the like.

    My father, at the death of his father, was

but six years of age; and he grew up,

litterally without education. He removed

from Kentucky to what is now Spencer county, Indi-

ana, in my eighth year. We reached our new home

about the time the State came into the Union. It

was a wild region, with many bears and other

wild animals still in the woods. There I grew

up. There were some schools, so called; but no

qualification was ever required of a teacher, beyond
"<u>readin, writin, and cipherin</u>"
~~reading, writing, and Arithmetic~~ to the Rule of
               supposed to understand latin,
Three. If a straggler ^ happened to sojourn in

The only photograph of Lincoln taken during the hectic year of
1859, this portrait was the work of Chicago's Samuel M. Fassett.
Mary Lincoln, who thought it "the best likeness she had ever seen
of her husband," took a copy with her to keep in the White House.

2

the neighborhood, he was looked upon as a wizzard— There was absolutely nothing to excite ambition for education. Of course when I came of age I did not know much— Still somehow, I could read, write, and cipher to the Rule of Three; but that was all— I have not been to school since— The little advance I now have upon this store of education, I have picked up from time to time under the pressure of necessity—

I was raised to farm work, which I continued till I was twenty-two— At twenty-one I came to Illinois, and passed the first year in Illinois Macon County— Then I got to New Salem (at that time in Sangamon, now in Menard County), where I remained a year as a sort of Clerk in a store— Then came the Black-Hawk war; and I was elected a Captain of Volunteers— a success which gave me more pleasure than any I have had since— I went the campaign, was elated, ran for the Legislature the same year (1832), and was beaten— the only time I ever have been beaten by the people— The next, and three succeeding biennial elections, I was elected to the Legislature— I was not a candidate afterwards. During this Legislative period I had studied law, and removed to Springfield to make practice it— In 1846 I was once elected to the Lower House of Congress— Was not a candidate for re-election— From 1849 to 1854, both the neighborhood, he was looked upon as a wizzard. There was absolutely nothing to excite ambition for education. Of course when I came of age ∧(I) did not know much. Still somehow, I could read, write, and cipher to the Rule of Three, but that was all. I have not been to school since. The little advance I now have upon this store of education, I have ~~have~~ picked up from time to time under the pressure of necessity.

I was raised to farm work, which I continued till I was twenty two. At twenty one I came to Illinois, and passed the first year in ~~Illinois~~ Macon County. Then I got ∧(to) New-Salem (~~then~~ ∧(at that time) in Sangamon, now in Menard County, where I remained a year as a sort of Clerk in a store. Then came the Black-Hawk war; and I was elected a Captain of Volunteers — a success which gave me more pleasure than any I have had since. I went the campaign, was elated, ran for the Legislature the same year (1832) and was beaten — the only time I ever have been beaten by the people — The next, and three succeeding biennial elections, I was elected to the Legislature. I was not a candidate afterwards. During this Legislative period I had studied law, and removed to Springfield to ~~make~~ practice it. In 1846 I was once elected to the lower House of Congress. Was not a candidate for re-election. From 1849 to 1854, both

Lincoln's beloved stepmother, Sarah Bush Johnston Lincoln, outlived "the best boy I ever saw" by four years.

Long estranged from his son, Lincoln's father, Thomas, could but "bunglingly sign his own name," his son later recalled unsympathetically.

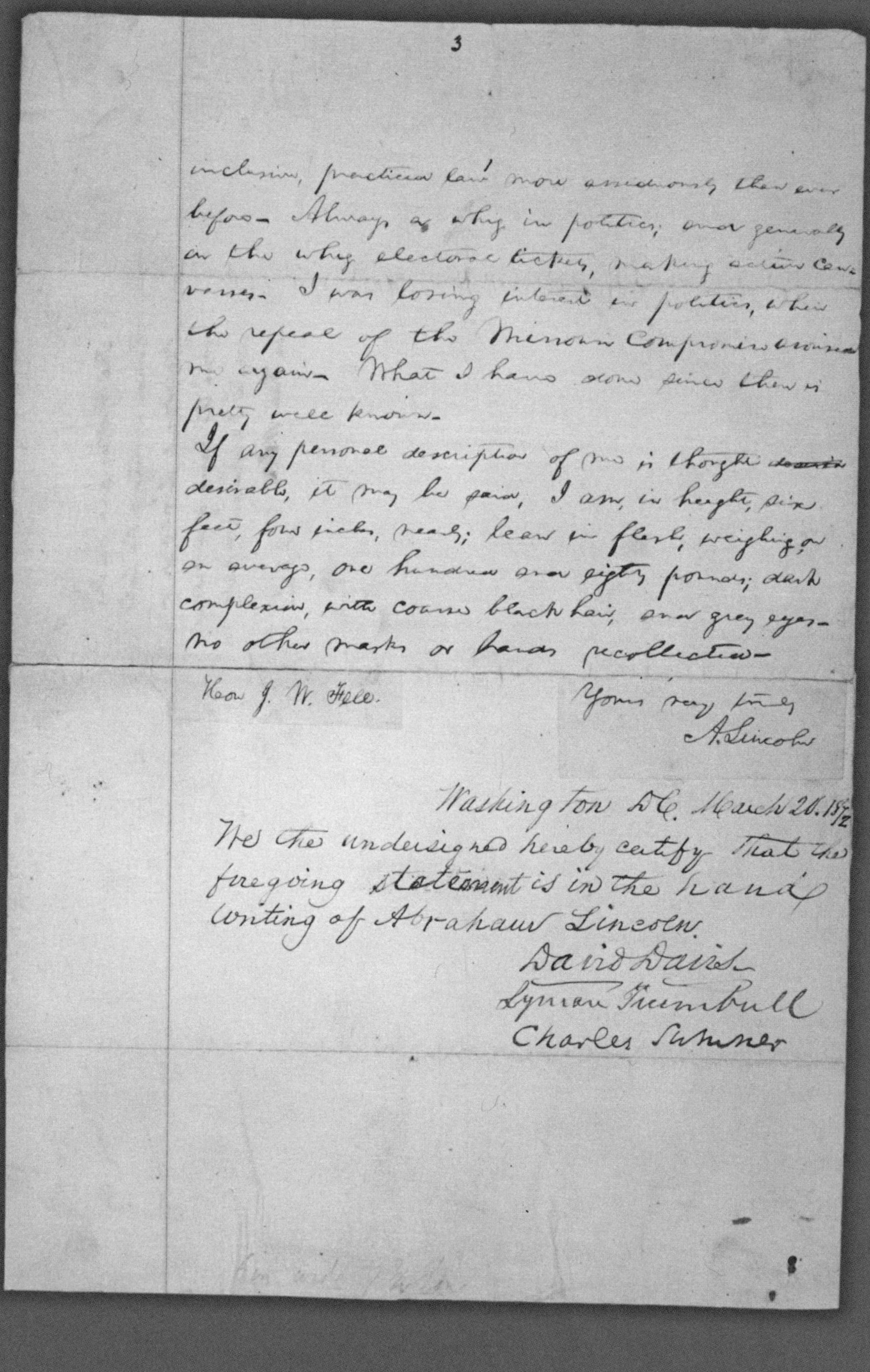

3

inclusive, practiced law more assiduously than ever before— Always a whig in politics; and generally on the whig electoral tickets, making active canvasses— I was losing interest in politics, when the repeal of the Missouri Compromise aroused me again— What I have done since then is pretty well known—

If any personal description of me is thought desirable, it may be said, I am, in height, six feet, four inches, nearly; lean in flesh, weighing, on an average, one hundred and eighty pounds; dark complexion, with coarse black hair, and grey eyes— No other marks or brands recollected—

Hon. J. W. Fell.   Yours very truly
                                     A. Lincoln

                    Washington D.C. March 20. 1872

We the undersigned hereby certify that the foregoing statement is in the hand writing of Abraham Lincoln.

                    David Davis
                    Lyman Trumbull
                    Charles Sumner

inclusive, practiced law more assiduously than ever before. Always a whig in politics, and generally on the whig electoral tickets, making active canvasses. I was losing interest in politics, when the repeal of the Missouri Compromise aroused me again. What I have done since then is pretty well known.

If any personal description of me is thought ~~desired~~ desirable, it may be said, I am, in height, six feet, four inches, nearly; lean in flesh, weighing, on an average, one hundred and eighty pounds; dark complexion, with coarse black hair, and grey eyes — no other marks or brands recollected.

Hon J. W. Fell   Yours very truly

                                        A. Lincoln

No one knows precisely when Lincoln posed for this, his first full-length photograph, but it may have been taken in early 1860 as a model for sculptor Leonard Wells Volk.

AUTOBIOGRAPHICAL SKETCH FOR THE *CHICAGO TRIBUNE*, JUNE 1860

A terse, private man, Lincoln also understood the power of his story. This, the most substantial memoir he ever wrote, aided his official campaign biographer in making the "railsplitter" from Illinois a national symbol of hard work and free labor. Here are the last two pages. *(Excerpt)*

13.

Mr L. thought the act of sending the boy an armed force to th among the Mexicans, was un-necessary, inasmuch as Mexico was in no way mo-lesting, or menacing the U. S. or the people there; and that it was unconstitutional, because the power of levying war is vested in Congress, and not in the President. He thought the princi-pal motive for the act, was to divert public attention from the surrender of "Fifty-four, forty, or fight" to Great Brittain, on the Oregon boundary question.

Mr L. was not a candidate for re-election—This was determined upon, and declared before he went to Washington, in accordance with an understanding, among whig friends, by which Col. Hardin, and Col. Baker had each previously served a single term in the same District— *

Upon his return from Congress he went to the practice of the law with greater earnest-ness than ever before— In 1852 he was upon the Scott electoral ticket, and did something in the way of canvassing, but owing to the hopelessness of the cause in th Illinois, he did less than in pre-vious presidential canvasses—

In 1854, his profession had almost superseded the thought of politics in his mind, when the repeal of the Missouri Compromise aroused him as he had never been before.

Mr. L. thought the act of sending ~~the troop~~ an armed force ~~to the~~ among the Mexicans, was <u>un-necessary</u>, inasmuch as Mexico was in no way mo-lesting, or menacing the U. S. or the people thereof; and that it was <u>unconstitutional</u>, because the power of levying war is vested in Congress, and not in the President. He thought the princi-pal motive for the act, was to divert public attention from the surrender of "Fifty-four, forty, or fight" to Great Brittain, on the Oregon boundary question.

Mr. L. was not a candidate for re-election. This was determined upon, and declared before he went to Washington, in accordance with an understanding ∧ among whig friends by which Col. Hardin, and Col. Baker had each previously served a single term in the same District.

Upon his return from Congress he went to the practice of the law with greater earnest-ness than ever before. In 1852 he was upon the Scott electoral ticket, and did something in the way of canvassing; but owing to the hopelessness of the cause in ~~th~~ Illinois, he did less than in pre-vious presidential canvasses.

In 1854. his profession had almost superseded the thought of politics in his mind, when the repeal of the Missouri compromise aroused him as he had never been before.

$\mathcal{D}$OUGLAS L. WILSON

For his own reasons, Abraham Lincoln was a most reluctant autobiographer, but as a presidential candidate, he had no choice but to provide biographical information for the use of friendly campaign biographers. The resulting manuscript is a fascinating study in restrained, highly selective self-disclosure, and nothing illustrates this more cogently than its conclusion. In an earlier, much briefer account, he had stopped in 1854: "I was losing interest in politics, when the repeal of the Missouri Compromise aroused me again. What I have done since then is pretty well known." This was doubtless his intention for the present manuscript, but it took an intriguing turn in execution. After emphasizing that the developments of 1854 "aroused him as he had never been before," he ends with this enigmatic sentence: "The State agricultural fair was at Springfield that year, and Douglas was announced to speak there." Clearly, this is only the beginning of an unfinished anecdote, but since this text was not written for publication, there was no need either to continue or revise. What he started to reveal but held back from describing had been, in fact, a life-changing experience: He had given the greatest speech of his life, had received a tumultuous and bipartisan response, and his political fortunes had been effectively turned around. ◄

14

In the autumn of that year he took the stump with no broader practical aim or object than to secure, if possible, the re-election of Hon Richard Yates to congress— His speeches at once attracted a more marked attention than they had ever before done— As the canvass proceeded, he was drawn to different parts of the state, outside of Mr. Yates' district— He did not abandon the law, but gave his attention, by turns, to that and politics— The State agricultural fair was at Springfield that year, and Douglas was ~~invited~~ announced to speak there.

In the autumn of that year he took the stump
with no broader practical aim or object that to
secure, if possible, the re-election of Hon Richard Yates to congress. His speeches at once
attracted a more marked attention than
they had ever before done. As the canvass proceeded, he was drawn to different
parts of the state, outside of Mr.
Yates' district. He did not abandon the
law, but gave his attention, by turns, to
that and politics. The State agricultural fair was at Springfield that year,
and Douglas was ~~announ~~ announced to
speak there.

On June 3, 1860, Alexander Hesler took the
photo on which these evocative etchings
(shown here in various states) were later
modeled. Hesler posed Lincoln inside the
Springfield State House, where the newly
anointed presidential nominee had opened a
temporary office.

Quite unlike modern campaigners, Lincoln spent his presidential campaign at home, where he largely stayed quiet. Having earlier labored to put his ideas into steadfast prose, Lincoln here refused a call to say more about the brewing crisis.

(copy)   Private & Confidential

Springfield, Ills. Oct. 29. 1860
Geo. D. Prentice, Esq
My dear Sir:

Yours of the 26th
is just received. Your suggestion
that I, in a certain event, shall write
a letter, setting forth my conservative
views and intentions, is certainly a very
worthy, one— But would it do any
good? If I were to labor a month,
I could not express my conservative
views and intentions more clearly and
strongly, than they are expressed in our plat-form,
and in my many speeches already
in print, and before the public. And
yet even you, who do occasionally speak
of me in terms of personal kindness, give
no prominence to these oft-repeated expressions
of conservative views and intentions;
but busy yourself with appeals to all
conservative men, to vote for Douglas—

(Copy)   Private & Confidential

          Springfield, Ills. Oct. 29. 1860

     Geo. D. Prentice, Esq

     My dear Sir:

               Yours of the 26th

is just received. Your suggestion

that I, in a certain event, shall write

a letter, setting forth my conservative

views and intentions, is certainly a very

worthy one. But would it do any

good? If I were to labor a month,

I could not express my conservative
                              clearly and
views and intentions more ∧ strongly, than

they are expressed in our plat-form,

and in my many speeches already

in print, and before the public. And

yet even you, who do occasionally speak

of me in terms of personal kindness, give

no prominence to these oft-repeated express-

ions of conservative views and intentions;

but busy yourself with appeals to all

conservative men, to vote for Douglas —

JONATHAN ALTER

Written only a week before Lincoln was elected president, this letter shows Lincoln trying to finesse a falling-out with an old friend. George D. Prentice was the powerful editor of the widely read *Louisville Journal,* which, like Lincoln, once backed Henry Clay and the Whigs. But now, Lincoln writes, Prentice was telling his border state readers "that you think I am the very worst man living." By intentionally overstating Prentice's ad hominem attacks, then suggesting that by contrast he himself bears no hard feelings, Lincoln plays on any guilt Prentice might feel for his harsh editorial tone. This gives Lincoln rhetorical room to deny the editor's request that he reassure Southerners with a statement of his "conservative views."

At first, Lincoln protests that these views have already been covered in the party platform and speeches. But at the end, he's more honest. While he regards "the majority" of Southerners as "good men" (more conciliation), he must also deal with "bad men" of "both North and South" who will twist his words and "fix upon me the character of timidity and cowardice." He doesn't trust the good faith of partisans on either side, doesn't believe they can be placated, and thus refuses to "put any weapons in their hands."

Lincoln didn't fully trust Prentice either. He didn't send the letter until after the election. But even while Prentice's sons served in the Confederate army, he consulted with President Lincoln on Kentucky affairs and helped keep Kentucky neutral. Lincoln had mastered the art of saying no nicely. ◄

to vote any way which can possibly
defeat me— thus impressing your readers to
believe that you think, I am the very
worst man living— If what I have
already said has failed to convince
you, no repetition of it would convince
you— The writing of your letter, now before me, gives assurance that you would
publish such a letter from me as you
suggest; but, till now, what reason
had I to suppose the Louisville Journal,
even, would publish a repetition of
that, which is already at its command and
which it does not press upon the public attention?

And, now my friend— for such I
esteem you personally— do not mis-
understand me— I have not decided
that I will not do substantially
what you suggest— I will not forbear
from doing so, merely, or practice,
pique— If I do finally abstain, it
will be because of apprehension
that it would do harm— For

to vote any way which can possibly

defeat me — thus ~~giving~~ your readers ~~to~~

^impressing^

~~believe~~ that you think, I am the very

worst man living. If what I have

already said has failed to convince

you, no repetition of it would convince

you. The writing of your letter, now be-

fore me, gives assurance that you would

publish such a letter from me as you

suggest; but, till now, what reason

had I ^to^ suppose the Louisville Journal,

even, would publish a <u>repetion</u>

of that ^which is^ already at it's command and

^press upon the public attention?^

which it does not ^ ~~publish?~~

   And, now my friend — for such I

esteem you personally — do not mis-

understand me. I have not decided

that I will not do substantially

what you suggest. I will not ~~abstain~~

^forbear^

~~from~~ doing so, merely on <u>punctilio</u>, ~~an~~

^and^

pluck. If I ^do^ finally abstain, it

will be because of apprehension

that it would do harm. For

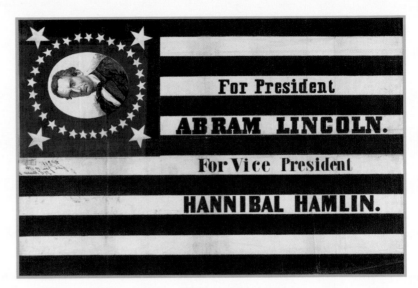

Stay-at-home candidate Lincoln was represented on the campaign trail by enthusiastic surrogates toting vivid flags like this one. The Illinoisan was still so little known that many allies initially mistook his first name.

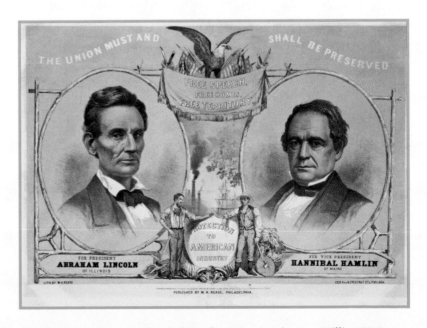

Lincoln and running mate Hannibal Hamlin appear together on a William H. Rease campaign poster from 1860. In truth, the running mates did not meet until after the election.

the good men of the South — and
I regard the majority of them as such —
I have no objection to repeat seventy
ty and seven times — But I have
bad men also to deal with both
North and South — men who are eager
for something new upon which to
base new misrepresentations — men who
would like to fighten me, or, at
least, to fix upon me the character
of timidity and cowardice — They would
seize upon almost any letter I could
write, as the being "awful coming down" — I
intend to keeping my eye upon these
gentlemen, and to not unnecessarily put
any weapons in their hands —
                    Yours very truly
                    A. Lincoln

the good men of the South — and regard the
I [???????????] majority of them as such —

I have no objection to repeat seven-

ty and seven times. But I have

<u>bad</u> men also to deal with both

North and South — men who are eager

for something new upon which to

base new misrepresentations — men who

would like to frighten me, ∧[or ???], at

least, ∧ to fix upon me the character

of timidity and cowardice. They would

seize upon almost any letter I could

write, as ∧ being an "<u>awful coming down</u>." I

intend ~~to~~ keeping my eye upon these

gentlemen, and to not unnecessarily put

any weapons in their hands.

        Yours very truly

          A. Lincoln

The 1860 political graphics were not all complimentary. In this racist anti-Republican lampoon, the uncomfortable-looking "rail candidate" tries straddling the vexing slavery issue, held aloft by a dehumanized black man and *New York Tribune* editor Horace Greeley.

[The following endorsement appears on the back:]

    <u>Confidential</u>
The within letter was written on the day of it's date, and, on re-flection, withheld till now. It expresses the views I still en-tertain.

        A. Lincoln

No one is sure who rendered this primitive sketch of Lincoln's February 11, 1861, farewell to Springfield—or when. No other period image exists. Linco proudly observed that despite the "large concourse of my fellow citizens" on hand at the depot to bid him goodbye, he "could recognize…almost all" of them.

Before leaving town, Mary posed with sons Willie (left) and Tad for Springfield photographer Preston Butler, a portrait later copied for *Frank Leslie's Illustrated Newspaper* The bucolic backdrop is fake, and the subjects look uncomfortable, but Mary proudly se copies to friends—even after Willie's February 1862 death.

Though he playfully waved away young Grace Bedell's suggestion that he grow whiskers to improve his appearance, Lincoln did just that shortly after his election. When he posed for this Samuel Alschuler photograph in Chicago on November 25, 1860, his new beard was barely a stubble.

C. S. German captured Lincoln with a fuller beard when he took this photograph in Springfield on January 13, 1861, at the request of visiting sculptor Thomas D. Jones.

Just two days before leaving Springfield, Lincoln posed for German for a final time—this time with his whiskers more cultivated, a new statesmanlike image now fully in place for his voyage to Washington.

FAREWELL TO SPRINGFIELD, FEBRUARY 11, 1861

With a long inaugural journey before him, and a daunting crisis awaiting, an anxious President-elect Lincoln bade farewell to his Springfield, Illinois, hometown. After delivering a heartfelt extemporaneous speech at the local depot to hundreds of neighbors, Lincoln wrote out—and vastly improved—his remarks for journalists who had already boarded his train, and missed its delivery.

My friends.

No one, not in my situation, can appreciate my feeling of sadness at this parting. To this place, and the kindness of these people, I owe every thing. Here I have lived a quarter of a century, and have passed from a young to an old man. Here my children have been born, and one is buried. I now leave, not knowing when, or whether ever, I may return, with a task before me greater than that which rested upon Washington. Without the assistance of that Divine Being, who ever attended him, I cannot succeed. With that assistance I cannot fail. Trusting in Him, who can go with me, and remain with you and be every where for good, let us confidently hope that all will yet be well. To His care commending you, as I hope in your prayers you will commend me, I bid you an affectionate farewell

My friends.

No one, not in my situation, can appreciate
my feeling of sadness, at this parting. To this
place, and the kindness of these people,
I owe every thing. Here I have been
a quarter of a century, and have
passed from a young to an old man.
Here my children have been born, and
one is buried. I now [~~????????~~]* leave,
not knowing when, or whether ever, I
may return, with a task before me greater
than that which rested upon Washington.
Without the assistance of that Divine
                    who
Being, ~~whom[?]~~ ever attended him, I
cannot succeed. With that assistance
I cannot fail. Trusting in Him, who
can go with me, and remain with
you and be everywhere for good, let
us confidently hope that all will yet be well.
To His care ⱡ commending you, as I
hope in your prayers you will commend me, I bid you an affectionate farewell.

*Lincoln's handwriting ends here; his private secretary, John G. Nicolay's,
begins; after three sentences, though the train continued rocking, Lincoln
resumed writing in pencil.

ᛋAM WATERSTON

On lined paper, Lincoln's careful
writing reminds one of a student
exercise. It's hard to imagine that this
was the work of a man on his way to
his presidential inauguration, that a
man so plain, even in penmanship,
could have come so far, and risen so
high. The handwriting makes the
simplicity of his diction stand out.

Looking back, we see simplicity as
a virtue, a talent, a power of Lincoln's.
But that simplicity was read very
differently at the time—as proof of
the man's inadequacy for the task
before him, by education, culture,
style, and breeding.

At first glance, this penciled scrap
of ephemera seems to support that
critical view. But not for long. We,
who are all too used to the hypocrisy
and wiggliness of politicians and their
talk, are treated here to the carefully
considered words of a man who meant
what he said, who meant to be
understood to mean what he meant,
and knew how to do it: a durable gem
of eloquence and condensed, packed-
down feeling.

The language, rooted in homespun, sings praises at heaven's gate.
To me, even in pencil, his writing still
makes the foundations of buildings
shake. ◄

Photograph by Mathew Brady gallery, Washington, ca. 1862.

Part Three

"WE CANNOT ESCAPE HISTORY"

1861-1863

"I doubt whether his words would be worth recording, even if I could remember them," the author Nathaniel Hawthorne reported dismissively after hearing Abraham Lincoln deliver a short speech in the White House in March 1862. Sneering that the president possessed "no bookish cultivation, no refinement," the novelist would concede only that "Uncle Abe" seemed armed with a "great deal of native sense." But even Lincoln's widely celebrated "delectable stories" smacked of "frontier freedom," Hawthorne complained, and were unfit for polite society.

How could one great writer have so badly misjudged another? The answer wasn't literary, but political. Hawthorne was a New England Democrat. Of course, neither the Yankee novelist nor other contemporary critics had ever glimpsed Lincoln's extraordinary—but private and unpublished—meditation on divine will, nor his condolence letter to a bereaved young woman named Fanny McCullough. Nor could they have anticipated the masterpieces yet to come from his pen.

Ironically, the most important document Lincoln ever wrote may have done the most during his lifetime to injure his reputation as a writer. Lincoln crafted the Emancipation Proclamation in meticulous legalese in anticipation of future court challenges to freedom. Its lack of soaring rhetoric disappointed many observers.

It took time, tragedy, and reassessment to modify Lincoln's reputation as both a statesman and a writer. And that would not come for years. Karl Marx, who had criticized Lincoln's work as "legal chicaneries and pettifogging stipulations," himself admitted of the "great and good man" he had failed to appreciate, "the world only discovered him a hero after he had fallen a martyr."

FIRST INAUGURAL ADDRESS, MARCH 4,1861

Lincoln's first inaugural address ends with perhaps the most famous illustration
of his literary mind in motion, as he revised a conciliatory closing paragraph (not shown on the
manuscript) that had been drafted by his secretary of state, William Seward.

The Chief Magistrate derives all his authority from the people, and they have conferred none upon him to fix terms for the separation of the States. The people themselves can do this *also* if they choose; but the executive, as such, has nothing to do with
it. His duty is to administer the present government, as it came to his hands, and to
transmit it, unimpaired by him, to his successor.

Why should there not be a patient confidence in the ultimate justice of the people?
Is there any better or equal hope, in the world? In our present differences, is either
party without faith *of being* in the right? If the Almighty Ruler of nations, with his eternal
truth and justice, be on *ou your side of the North, or on yours of the South,* that truth and that justice, will surely
prevail, by the judgment of this great tribunal, the American people.

By the frame of the government under which we live, this same people have wisely
given their public servants but little power for mischief; and have, with equal wisdom,
provided for the return of that little to their own hands at very short intervals.
While the people *retain their vertue, and vigilence, no administration* by any extreme of wickedness or folly, can very seriously injure the
government, in the short space of four years.

My countrymen, one and all, *think calmly and* well, upon this whole sub-
ject. Nothing valuable can be lost by taking time. If there be an object to *hurry* any of you, in hot haste,
to a step which you would never take *deliberately*, that object will be frustrated by
taking time; but no good object can be frustrated by it. Such of you as are now
dissatisfied, still have the old Constitution unimpaired, and, on the sensitive point, the
laws of your own framing under it; while the new administration will have no immediate power, if it would, to change either. If it were admitted that you who are
dissatisfied, hold the right side in the dispute, there still is no single good reason for
precipitate action. Intelligence, patriotism, Christianity, and a firm reliance on Him,
who has never yet forsaken this favored land, are still competent to adjust, in the best
way, all our present difficulty.

In *your* hands, my dissatisfied fellow countrymen, and not in *mine*, is the momentous issue of civil war. The government will not assail *you*.
You can have no conflict, without being yourselves the aggressors. *You* have no oath
registered in Heaven to destroy the government, while *I* shall have the most solemn one
to "preserve, protect and defend" it.

*I am loth to close. We are not enemies,
but friends— We must not be enemies. Though passion may
have strained, it must not break our bonds of affection.
The mystic chords of memory, stretching from every battle-
field, and patriot grave, to every living heart and hearth-
stone, all over this broad land, will yet swell the cho-
rus of the Union, when again touched, as surely they will
be, by the better angels of our nature.*

The Chief Magistrate derives all his authority from the people, and they have conferred none upon him to fix terms for the separation of the States. The people themselves can do this ∧*also* if they choose; but the executive, as such, has nothing to do with it. His duty is to administer the present government, as it came to his hands, and to transmit it, unimpaired by him, to his successor.

Why should there not be a patient confidence in the ultimate justice of the people? Is there any better, or equal hope, in the world? In our present differences, is either party without faith ∧*of being* in the right? If the Almighty Ruler of nations, with his eternal truth and justice, be on ∧*on your side of the North, or on yours of the South,* ~~our side, or on yours,~~ that truth, and that justice, will surely prevail, by the judgment of this great tribunal, the American people.

By the frame of the government under which we live, this same people have wisely given their public servants but little power for mischief: and have, with equal wisdom, provided for the return of that little to their own hands at very short intervals. While the people ∧*retain their virtue, and vigilence, no administration* ~~remain patient, and true to themselves, no man, even in the presidential chair~~ ∧*can,* by any extreme of wickedness or folly, can very seriously injure the government, in the short space of four years.

My countrymen, one and all, ∧*think calmly and* ~~take time and think~~ *well*, upon this whole subject. Nothing valuable can be lost by taking time. ~~Nothing worth preserving is either breaking or burning~~. If there be an object to *hurry* any of you, in hot haste, to a step which you would never take *deliberately*, that object will be frustrated by taking time; but no good object can be frustrated by it. Such of you as are now dissatisfied, still have the old Constitution unimpaired, and, on the sensitive point, the laws of your own framing under it; while the new administration will have no immediate power, if it would, to change either. If it were admitted that you who are dissatisfied, hold the right side in the dispute, there still is no single good reason for precipitate action. Intelligence, patriotism, Christianity, and a firm reliance on Him, who has never yet forsaken this favored land, are still competent to adjust, in the best way, all our present difficulty.

In *your* hands, my dissatisfied fellow countrymen, and not in *mine*, is the momentous issue of civil war. The government will not assail *you*. ~~unless you *first* assail *it*.~~ You can have no conflict, without being yourselves the aggressors. *You* have no oath registered in Heaven to destroy the government, while *I* shall have the most solemn one to "preserve, protect and defend" it. ~~*You* can forbear, the *assault* upon it; *I* can *not* shrink from the *defense* of it. With *you*, and not with *me*, is the solemn question of "Shall it be peace, or a sword?"~~ I am loth to close. We are not enemies,

friends. We must not be enemies. Though passion may

strained, it must not break our bonds of affection.

mystic chords of memorys, streching from every battle-

, and patriot grave, to every living heart and hearth-

, all over this broad land, will yet swell the cho-

of the Union, when again touched, as surely they will

y the better angels of our nature.

The Civil War had not yet begun. In his draft of his first inaugural address, President-elect Lincoln had planned to conclude with a message to his "dissatisfied friends" in the South that the choice of "peace or the sword" was in their hands, and not in his. William Seward, whom Lincoln had beaten for the Republican nomination and after the election had appointed secretary of state, suggested in a letter that this note of defiance be tempered with "a note of fraternal affection," and submitted language for the penultimate paragraphs:

I close. We are not, we must not be, aliens or enemies, but fellow countrymen and brethren. Although passion has strained our bonds of affection too hardly, they must not, I am sure they will not, be broken. The mystic chords which, proceeding from so many battlefields and so many patriotic graves, pass through all the hearts and all hearths in this broad continent of ours, will yet again harmonize in their ancient music when breathed upon by the guardian angel of the nation.

Lincoln accepted Seward's idea of seeking to evoke the sentimental ties that could help bind the nation together, and he used Seward's musical metaphor as well. But he rewrote the suggested passage, lifting it from oratory to poetry.

Do users of political language today make that kind of effort to persuade and inspire? I think not. If they did, would it work? Styles change with the times, and Seward's florid style may seem excessive to us now, but Lincoln's improvement produced a soaring simplicity that I believe has what we now call impact. ◄

Lincoln boldly appointed what historian Doris Kearns Goodwin called a "team of rivals" to fill his cabinet, but resisted when Secretary of State William H. Seward attempted to co-opt his authority. As the untested incoming president had confided earlier, "I can't afford to let Seward take the first trick."

Executive Mansion
April 1. 1861

Hon: W. H. Seward:
   My dear Sir:

      Since parting with you I have
been considering your paper dated this day, and
entitled "Some thoughts for the President's consideration". The first proposition in it is.

"1." We are at the end of a month's administration, and yet without a policy, either
domestic or foreign".

At the beginning of that month, in the inaugural, I said "The power confided to me will be
used to hold, occupy, and possess the property
and places belonging to the government, and
to collect the duties, and imports". This
had your distinct approval at the time; and,
taken in connection with the order I immediately gave General Scott, directing him to em-
ploy every means in his power to strengthen and
hold the forts, comprises the exact domestic
policy you now urge, with the single exceptio

Executive Mansion

April 1, 1861

Hon: W. H. Seward:

My dear Sir:

Since parting with you I have

been considering your paper dated this day, and

entitled "Some thoughts for the President's con-

sideration." The first proposition in it is,

"1st. We are at the end of a month's ad-

ministration, and yet without a policy, either

domestic or foreign."

At the <u>beginning</u> of that month, in the inauger-

al, I said "The power confided to me will be

used to hold, occupy and possess the property

and places belonging to the government, and

to collect the duties, and imports." This

had your distinct approval at the time; and,

taken in connection with the order I immedi-

ately gave General Scott, directing him to em-

ploy every means in his power to strengthen and

hold the forts, comprises the exact domestic

policy you now urge, with the single exception,

PRESIDENT GEORGE H. W. BUSH

In due course, President Lincoln's hands, enlarged by his years of splitting rails and plowing fields, proved big enough to hold the Union together. Yet from the very first of his administration, this icon of principled American leadership was forced to justify himself and his actions even to an intemperate member of his own cabinet.

His rivalry with Seward is long-since acknowledged; but to me what this early letter from our sixteenth president serves to underscore is the innate grace and humility with which Lincoln served— while at the same time forcefully asserting, with even a modicum of panache, the limited powers of the Executive under our Constitution. (Note the underlined "I" for emphasis on the third line of page three.)

Like others to assume the presidency, I was keen to learn from precedence—from the wisdom and, yes, the mistakes of those who had preceded me into high office. I am not alone in that, from Lincoln, I drew plain lessons in propriety, and reserve, and respect for that unique institution into which so many American hopes and dreams have been vested.

President Lincoln once notably spoke of being "driven to (his) knees" by the weight of the decisions only a president can face, and the realization that only a merciful Creator could abide his fondest wish to see the Union preserved.

(continued)

on, that it does not propose to abandon Fort
Sumpter—

Again, I do not perceive how the re-in
forcement of Fort Sumpter would be done
on a slavery, or party issue, while that
of Fort Pickens would be on a more national, and patriotic one.

The news received yesterday in regard
to St. Domingo, certainly brings a new item within
the range of our foreign policy; but up to that
time we have been preparing Circulars, and
instructions to Ministers, and the like, all
in perfect harmony, without even a suggestion
tion that we had no foreign policy.

Upon your closing propositions, that "whatever policy
we adopt, there must be an energetic prosecution of it"

"For this purpose it must be somebody's
business to pursue and direct it incessantly".

"Either the President must do it himself,
and be all the while active in it, or"

"Devolve it on some member of his Cabinet

"Once adopted, debates on it must end,
and all agree and abide". I remark that
if this must be done, I must do it. When
a general line of policy is adopted, I apprehend there is no danger of its being changed
without good reason, or continuing to be
a subject of unnecessary debate; still,
upon points arising in its progress, I wish,
and suppose I am entitled to have the
advice of all the Cabinet—

Your Obt. Servt.

A. Lincoln

on, that it does not propose to abandon Fort Sumpter.

Again, I do not perceive how the re-inforcement of Fort Sumpter would be done on a slavery, or party issue, while that of Fort Pickens would be on a more national, and patriotic one.

The news received yesterday in regard to St. Domingo, certainly brings a new item [within] the range of our foreign policy; but up to that time we have been preparing circulars, and instructions to ministers, and the like, all in perfect harmony, without even a suggestion that we had no foreign policy. Upon your closing propositions, that "whatever policy we adopt, there must be an energetic prosecution of it"

"For this purpose it must be somebody's business to pursue and direct it incessantly"

"Either the President must do it himself, and be all the while active in it, or"

"Devolve it on some member of his cabinet"

"Once adopted, debates on it must end, and all agree and abide" I remark that if this must be done, I must do it. When a general line of policy is adopted, I apprehend there is no danger of its being changed without good reason, or continuing to be a subject of unnecessary debate; still, upon points arising in its progress, I wish, and suppose I am entitled to have the advice of all the Cabinet.

Your Obt. Servt.

A. Lincoln

Still, as we reflect on the remarkable circumstances of his service, it is we, in turn, who should be driven to our knees in gratitude that such a man of fortitude, and quiet conviction, was elevated in due process to deliver our republic from its hour of maximum peril.

Awkward, ungainly perhaps, but in the end also unyielding, Abraham Lincoln's intellect and reason were the rock, the foundation, upon which a young and searching nation was able to rise above its gravest threat to truly become the "last best, hope of earth." ◄

Lincoln believed his Secretary of State, William H. Seward, "seemed to share the fate of the ancient picture placed by the painter in the market-house to be retouched by all caviling critics."

MESSAGE TO CONGRESS, JULY 4, 1861

Lincoln's first crucial message to Congress—delivered to a special session called for Independence Day—marshaled the national will for war, and began an effort to define that war. "This is essentially a people's contest," he argued. Praised in the North, it convinced one Baltimore newspaper that Lincoln was "the equal, in despotic wickedness, of Nero…." *(Excerpt)*

and the authority of the people?

This is essentially a people's contest. On the side of the Union, it is a struggle for maintaining in the world, that form, and substance of government, whose leading object is to elevate the condition of men— to lift artificial weights from all shoulders—

to clear the paths of laudable pursuit for all— to afford all an unfettered start, and a fair chance, in the race of life— Yielding to partial, and temporary departures, from necessity, this is the leading object of the government for whose existence we contend—

I am most happy to believe that the plain people understand, and appreciate this. It is worthy of note, that while in this, the government's hour of trial, large numbers of those in the Army and Navy, who have been favored with the offices, have resigned, and played false to the very hand which had pampered them, not one common soldier, or common sailor has deserted his flag—

This is essentially a people's contest. On the

side of the Union, it is a struggle for main-

taining in the world, that form, and sub-

stance of government, whose leading object

is to elevate the condition of men — to lift

artificial weights from all shoulders —

to clear the paths of laudable purs-
                              unfettered
uit for all — to afford all an ~~even~~

start, and a fair chance, in the race

of life. Yielding to partial, and tempo-

rary departures, from necessity, this ∧ is ~~I hold~~

~~to be~~ the leading object of the govern-

ment for whose existence we contend.

  I am most happy to believe that the

plain people understand, and appreciate

this. It is worthy of note, that while in this,

the government's hour of trial, large numbers

of those in the Army and Navy, who

have been favored with the offices, have

resigned, and played false to the very hand

which had pampered them, not one common

soldier, or common sailor has deserted his flag.

PRESIDENT GEORGE W. BUSH

On July 4, 1861, Abraham Lincoln convened a special session of Congress unlike any other in history. In the preceding months, eleven states had seceded from the Union. Rebel forces had fired on Fort Sumter. And now an anxious nation looked to the prairie lawyer from Springfield to rise to the challenge.

In his Independence Day message to Congress, Lincoln answered his skeptics with resolve and eloquence. Drawing on his knowledge of history, he refuted the argument for secession. He asked Congress to provide the resources needed to preserve the Union. And to those who might question the cost, he wrote, "A right result, at this time, will be worth more to the world, than ten times the men, and ten times the money."

From the beginning, Lincoln understood that the outcome of America's Civil War would reverberate far beyond America's borders. In his message, Lincoln described the battle to save the Union as a struggle for the future of democracy around the world. As the years passed, Americans would grow to realize the wisdom of their president's words. And as slaves claimed their God-given right to freedom, America would grow into the more perfect union that Lincoln had always envisioned.

(continued)

Greater honor is due to those officers who remain true, despite the example of their treacherous associates; but the greater honor, and most important fact of all, is, the unanimous firmness of the common soldiers and common sailors. To the last man, they have successfully resisted the traitorous efforts of those, whose commands, but an hour before, they obeyed as absolute law. This is the patriotic instinct of plain people. They understand, without an argument, that the destroying the government which was made by Washington, means no good to them.

Our popular government has often been called an experiment. Two points in it, our people have already settled— the successful establishing, and the successful administering of it— One still remains — the successful maintainance of it, against a formidable attempt to overthrow it. It is now for them to demonstrate to the world that those who can fairly carry

Greater honor is due to those officers who

remain true, despite the example of their

treacherous associates; but the greatest honor,

and most important fact ∧ is, the unanimous
                          of all

firmness of the common soldiers and ∧ sail-
                                   common

ors. To the last man, they ∧ successfully
                            have

resisted the traitorous efforts of those, who-

se commands, but an hour before, they

obeyed as absolute law. This is the

patriotic instinct of the plain people. They

understand, without an argument, that

the destroying the government which was

made by Washington, means no good

to them.

   Our popular government has often been call-

ed an experiment. Two points in it, our peo-

ple have already settled — the success-

ful <u>establishing,</u> and the successful

<u>administering</u> of it. One still remains

— the successful <u>maintainance</u> of it,

against a formidable attempt to overthrow

it. It is now for them to demonstrate to

the world that those who can fairly carry

   Lincoln's Message to Congress is remembered for describing the Civil War as "a people's contest." And thanks to the leadership of America's sixteenth president, government of the people, by the people, for the people prevailed. ◄

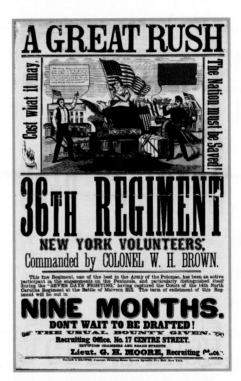

This early broadside promoting nine-month enlistments stressed patriotism but hinted darkly—and accurately—at future conscription.

an election, can also suppress a rebellion—
that those who can not carry an election, can not destroy the government.
— that ballots are the rightful, and
peaceful, successor of bullets; and that
when ballots have fairly, and consti-
tutionally, decided, there can be no successful appeal, back to bullets. Such
will be a great lesson of peace, teaching
men that what they can not take by an
election, neither can they take it by a
war— teaching all the folly of being the
beginners of a war

Lest there be some uneasiness in the minds
of candid men, as to what is to be the course
of the government, towards the southern states,
after the rebellion shall have been sup-
pressed, the executive deems it proper to say
it will be his purpose, then as ever, to be
guided by the Constitution, and the laws;
and that he probably will have no different understanding of the powers, and
duties of the Federal government, relative to
the rights of the States, and the people, under the Constitution, than that expressed in
the inaugural address—

an election, can also suppress a rebellion —
that those who can <u>not</u> carry an election, can not destroy the government.
— that ballots are the rightful, and
peaceful, successor of bullets; and that
when ballots have fairly, and consti-
tutionally, decided, there can be no successful appeal, back to bullets. Such
will be a great lesson of peace, teaching
men that what they can not take by an
election, neither can they take it by a
war — teaching all the folly of being the
beginners of a war

Lest there be some uneasiness in the minds
of candid men, as to what is to be the course
of the government, towards the Southern states,
<u>after</u> the rebellion shall have been sup-
pressed, the executive deems it proper to say
it will be his purpose, then as ever, to be
guided by the Constitution, and the laws;
and that he probably will have no different understanding of the powers, and
duties of the Federal government, relative to
the rights of the States, and the people, under the Constitution, than that expressed in
the inaugural address.

The attack on Fort Sumter, the federal garrison guarding Charleston harbor, ignited war but also inspired artists—and may have elevated morale, not sapped it. When the fort's badly damaged flag was returned to New York, it was displayed to rally civilians and inspire departing troops.

The resulting damage to Fort Sumter's American flag ignited what was called "flag mania" in the North, an outpouring of banners and artistic renderings designed to fan patriotic flames and inspire a commitment to armed response. This Currier & Ives print invoked both Union martyrs and God's blessings.

Lincoln seldom combined legalese and poetry in a single document, but in revoking a Civil War
general's precipitant order confiscating local slaves—a right Lincoln held to himself—
the president ingeniously appealed to both the law and the heart. *(Excerpt)*

By the President of the United States of America.

A Proclamation.

Whereas there appears in the public prints,
what purports to be a proclamation, of Major
General Hunter, in the words and figures
following, towit:

> Headquarters Department of the South,
> Hilton Head, S. C., May 9, 1862.
> General Orders No. 11—The three States of
> Georgia, Florida and South Carolina, comprising
> the military department of the south, having de-
> liberately declared themselves no longer under
> the protection of the United States of America,
> and having taken up arms against the said United
> States, it becomes a military necessity to declare
> them under martial law. This was accordingly
> done on the 25th day of April, 1862. Slavery and
> martial law in a free country are altogether incom-
> patible; the persons in these three States—Geor-
> gia, Florida and South Carolina—heretofore held
> as slaves, are therefore declared forever free.
> (Official)   DAVID HUNTER,
>   Major General Commanding.
> Ed. W. Smith, Acting Assistant General.

And whereas the same is producing some ex-
citement, and misunderstanding: Therefore

I, Abraham Lincoln, president of
the United States, proclaim and declare,
that the government of the United States, had no knowledge, information, or belief, of an intention on the part of General Hunter to issue such a proclamation;
nor has it yet, any authentic information
that the document is genuine And further,
that neither General Hunter, nor any other
commander, or person, has been expressly, or

By the President of the United States of America.

A Proclamation.

Whereas there appears in the public prints,

what purports to be a proclamation, of Major

General Hunter, in the words and figures

following, towit:

Headquarters Department of the South,}
Hilton Head, S.C., May 9, 1862.}
General Orders No. 11.— The three States of
Georgia, Florida and South Carolina, comprising
the military department of the south, having deliberately declared themselves no longer under
the protection of the United States of America,
and having taken up arms against the said United
States, it becomes a military necessity to declare
them under martial law. This was accordingly
done on the 25th day of April, 1862. Slavery and
martial law in a free country are altogether incom-
patible; the persons in these three States—Georgia, Florida and South Carolina— heretofore held
as slaves, are therefore declared forever free.
(Official)   DAVID HUNTER,
                        Major General Commanding.
ED. W. SMITH, Acting Assistant General.

And whereas the same is producing some ex-

citement, and misunderstanding: therefore

I, Abraham Lincoln, president of

the United States, proclaim and declare,

that the government of the United Sta-

tes, had no knowledge, information, or be-

lief, of an intention on the part of Gen-

eral Hunter to issue such a proclamation;

nor has it yet, any authentic information

that the document is genuine. And further,

that neither General Hunter, nor any other

commander, or person, has been expressly, or

FRANK J. WILLIAMS

When Lincoln's friend, Major General David Hunter, ordered slaves in Georgia, Florida, and South Carolina "forever free," the President learned about it from the press.

Lincoln revoked the initiative at once, telling Secretary of the Treasury Salmon P. Chase: "No commanding general shall do such a thing, upon my responsibility, without consulting me."

The revocation showed the lawyer/president at his best. Drafted as a legal document, the commander in chief even pasted Hunter's order from a newspaper onto the center of the first page—shown here—then explained his determination to override it. Any such exercise of power, "I reserve to myself." The emancipator-in-waiting declares that emancipation cannot yet be undertaken at this time (though by July, he had drafted an Emancipation Proclamation of his own). For now, he again urges gradual, compensated emancipation, asserting the plan "makes common cause for a common object, casting no reproaches on any."

And he ends with a flourish, looking not to Hunter's recent indiscretion but to his own plans for "the vast future": "The change it contemplates would come gently as the dews of heaven…. Will you not embrace it? So much good has not been done, by one effort, in all past time, as in the providence of God, it is now your high privilege to do."

This is Abraham Lincoln at his best— judicious, tough, eloquent, and yet open to mediation, using "all the…means of persuasion…." ◄

Even after he had composed his Emancipation Proclamation, Lincoln publicly maintained—in this enigmatic reply to the irascible newspaperman Horace Greeley—his primary commitment to the preservation of the Union and the secondary consideration of slavery. This was, he said, his official duty, though not necessarily his personal wish.

Executive Mansion,

Washington, August 22, 1862.

Hon. Horace Greely:

Dear Sir =

= I have just read yours of the 19th addressed to myself through the New-York Tribune— If there be in it any statements, or assumptions of fact, which I may know to be erroneous, I do not, now, and here, controvert them. If there be in it any inferences which I may believe to be falsely drawn, I do not now and here, argue against them. If there be perceptable in it an impatient and dictatorial tone, I waive it in deference to an old friend, whose heart I have always supposed to be right—

As to the policy I "seem to be pursuing" as you say, I have not meant to leave any one in doubt—

I would save the Union. I would save it the shortest way under the Constitution. The

Executive Mansion,

Washington, August 22, 1862.

Hon. Horace Greely:

Dear Sir -

-I have just read yours of the

19th addressed to myself through the New-

York Tribune. If there be in it any statements,

or assumptions of fact, which I may know to be

erroneous, I do not, now and here, controvert

them. If there be in it any inferences which

I may believe to be falsely drawn, I do not

now and here, argue against them. If there

be perceptable in it an impatient and dic-

tatorial tone, I waive it in deference to an

old friend, whose heart I have always sup-

posed to be right.

As to the policy I "seem to be pursuing" as you

say, I have not meant to leave any one in

doubt.

I would save the Union. I would save it

the shortest way under the Constitution. The

DAVID W. BLIGHT

In the late summer of 1862 Lincoln faced steady criticism for Union military failures in Virginia and for his apparent indecision on the issue of slave emancipation. On August 20, Horace Greeley, the founder and editor of the *New York Tribune,* the most influential newspaper in America, published a nine-part indictment of Lincoln under the title, "The Prayer of Twenty Millions." Raining a hail of invective on Lincoln, Greeley demanded that he enforce the Second Confiscation Act, passed by Congress the previous month and authorizing the president to free the slaves as enemy property.

Beautiful in its brevity and gracious in tone, Lincoln's famous, enigmatic response of August 22, published in the pro-Union but also pro-slavery *National Intelligencer,* was a deft work of political propaganda; indeed it may have been intentionally misleading. After all, on July 22 Lincoln had informed his cabinet that he intended to issue an emancipation order. He was waiting only for a military victory, so as to avoid the appearance of desperation.

After a cordial opening paragraph, Lincoln made his case in two remarkable paragraphs that people have chosen to read in vastly different ways. Was this the emancipator in the making, awaiting his moment of truth?

(continued)

sooner the national authority can be restored, the nearer the Union will be "the Union as it was". ~~Broken eggs can never be mended, and the longer the breaking proceed, the more will be broken~~ — If there be, those who would not save the Union, unless they could at the same time save slavery, I do not agree with them — If there be those who would not save the Union unless they could at the same time destroy slavery, I do not agree with them, My paramount object in this struggle is to save the Union, and is not either to save or to destroy slavery — If I could save the Union without freeing any slave I would do, it, and if I could save it by freeing all the slaves I would do it; and if I could save it by freeing some and leaving others alone I would also do that — What I do about slavery, and the colored race, I do because I believe it helps, to save the Union;

sooner the national authority can be restored, the nearer the Union will be "the Union as it was." ~~Broken eggs can never be mended, and~~ ~~the longer the breaking process, the more will~~ ~~be broken~~. If there be ∧ ~~any~~ those who would not save the Union, unless they could at the same time <u>save</u> slavery, I do not agree with them. If there be ~~any~~ those who would not save the Union unless they could at the same time <u>destroy</u> slavery, I do not agree with them.

My paramount object in this struggle <u>is</u> to save the Union, and is <u>not</u> either to save or to destroy slavery. If I could save the Union without freeing <u>any</u> slave I would do, it, and if I could save it by freeing <u>all</u> the slaves I would do it; and if I could save it by freeing some and leaving others alone I would also do that. What I do about slavery, and the colored race, I do because I believe it helps to save the Union;

Or was this the conservative Republican who preferred to restore the Union without destroying slavery? Or was it both the moderate—now moved by events and older moral convictions about slavery—and the wily politician educating the public up to its historical duty? The one thing he made clear is that the "paramount object...the cause" was to save the Union. To Lincoln, though, emancipation had become both a means and an end.

In its context the letter demonstrates that both Lincoln and Greeley eventually agreed that defeat of the Confederacy and emancipation were now mutually necessary and dependent. The sentence edited out by the *National Intelligencer* contained the homespun metaphor of "broken eggs." He had taken his time, but Lincoln was now willing to break as many eggs as it took to crush the rebellion.

(continued)

New York Tribune editor Horace Greeley at first thought Lincoln "true and right, but not a Jackson or Clay."

and what I forbear, I forbear because I
do _not_ believe it would help to save the
Union— I shall do _less_ whenever I shall be=
lieve what I am doing hurts the cause, and
I shall do _more_ whenever I shall believe
doing more will help the cause— I shall try
to correct errors when shown to be errors; and I
shall adopt new views so fast as they shall
appear to be true views—

I have here stated my purpose according
to my view of _official_ duty; and I intend
no modification of my oft-expressed per-
sonal wish that all men everywhere could
be free—

Yours,

A. Lincoln

and what I forbear, I forbear because I do <u>not</u> believe it would help to save the Union. I shall do <u>less</u> whenever I shall believe what I am doing hurts the cause, and I shall do <u>more</u> whenever I shall believe doing more will help the cause. I shall try to correct errors when shown to be errors; and I shall adopt new views so fast as they shall appear to be true views.

I have here stated my purpose according to my view of <u>official</u> duty; and I intend no modification of my oft-expressed <u>personal</u> wish that all men everywhere could be free.

Yours,

A. Lincoln

In the final sentence Lincoln also made the distinction between his *"official duty"* and his *"personal wish"* that all could be free. Lincoln's multilayered temperament was a house with many doors. The Greeley letter, like few other works in Lincoln's writings, demonstrates how many choices we have in entering that house. ◄

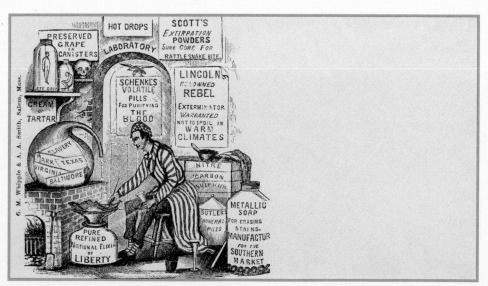

Grinding his pills and potions, "pharmacist" Lincoln searches for the perfect cure to restore the country's health. Crude so-called patriotic envelopes like this one were immensely popular on the home front.

The thorny question of God's will in relation to the Civil War nagged at Lincoln as the conflict mounted. In this private note, discovered only after his death, he staked out a theologically rigorous position. Notice how the tone changes in the second half, after the one strike-out (the word "this") when he moved from declaring his certainties to wrestling with the ultimate question.

The will of God prevails— In great contests each party claims to act in accordance with the will of God. Both may be, and one must be wrong. God can not be for, and against the same thing at the same time. In the present civil war it is quite possible that God's purpose is something different from the purpose of either party— and yet the human instrumentalities, working just as they do, are of the best adaptation to effect ~~this~~ his purpose. I am almost ready to say this is probably true— that God wills this contest, and wills that it shall not end yet— By his mere quiet power, on the minds of the now contestants, He could have either saved or destroyed the Union without a human contest— Yet the contest began— And having begun He could give the final victory to either side any day— Yet the contest proceeds—

The will of God prevails. In great contests each party claims to act in accordance with the will of God. Both <u>may</u> be, and one <u>must</u> be wrong. God can not be <u>for</u>, and <u>against</u> the same thing at the same time. In the present civil war it is quite possible that God's purpose is something different from the purpose of either party — and yet the human instrumentalities, working just as they do, are of the best adaptation to effect ~~this~~ His purpose. I am almost ready to say this is probably true — that God wills this contest, and wills that it shall not end yet. By his mere quiet power, on the minds of the now contestants, He could have either <u>saved</u> or <u>destroyed</u> the Union without a human contest. Yet the contest began. And having begun He could give the final victory to either side any day. Yet the contest proceeds.

℗RESIDENT JIMMY CARTER

There is no addressee or context given that precipitated this memorandum, but it is very troubling to me. Although the detached objectivity and humor of Abraham Lincoln are clear in his assessment of the "will of God," his strong insinuation is that it was God's unfathomable will that caused the beginning and continuation of the horrendous War between the States.

There is no doubt that many conflicts are initiated because combatants are convinced that they are implementing particular and misguided interpretations of Christianity, Islam, Judaism, or other prevalent religions and that they are acting on behalf of the Almighty. In order to arouse or strengthen support, it is a major responsibility for political and military leaders to inculcate both soldiers and civilians with this sense of self-righteousness. At least in this brief presentation, Lincoln refrained from doing so. Rather than exalt the unique morality of his own cause as commander in chief of the Union army, Lincoln acknowledges the legitimacy, or inevitability, of both sides claiming to be acting in good faith.

He ignores the fact that the tragic combat might have been avoided altogether, and that the leaders of both sides, overwhelmingly Christian, were violating a basic premise of their belief as followers of the Prince of Peace. His subtle purpose may have been to disparage the fervent proponents of this faith.

A legitimate question for historians is how soon the blight of slavery would have been terminated peacefully in America, as in Great Britain and other civilized societies. ◄

PRELIMINARY EMANCIPATION PROCLAMATION, SEPTEMBER 22, 1862

Lincoln wrote—and pasted together (one glued section on page 108 seems to bear his fingerprint!)—
this history-altering preliminary Emancipation Proclamation sometime in September 1862.
Later donated to a New York charity fair, it was eventually acquired and preserved by the state.
It is the only surviving copy of Lincoln's most important document in his own hand; the manuscript
of the final proclamation burned in the Chicago fire.

By the President of the
United States of America
A Proclamation.

I, Abraham Lincoln, President of the United
States of America, and Commander-in-Chief
of the Army and Navy thereof, do hereby proclaim and declare that hereafter, as heretofore, the war will be prosecuted for the object of practically restoring the constitutional relation between the United States, and each
of the states, and the people thereof, in which
states that relation is, or may be, suspended, or
disturbed.

That it is my purpose, upon the next meeting
of Congress to again recommend the adoption of
a practical measure tendering pecuniary aid to
the free acceptance or rejection of all slave-
states, so called, the people whereof may not then
be in rebellion against the United States, and
which states, may then have voluntarily adopted, or thereafter may voluntarily adopt, immediate, or gradual abolishment of slavery within their respective limits; and that the effort
to colonize persons of African descent, upon this
continent, or elsewhere, will be continued.

By the President of the

United States of America

A Proclamation.

I, Abraham Lincoln, President of the United

States of America, and Commander-in-Chief

of the Army and Navy thereof, do hereby pro-

claim and declare that hereafter, as hereto-

fore, the war will be prossecuted for the ob-

ject of practically restoring the constitutional re-

lation between the United States, and each

of the states, and the people thereof, in which

states that relation is, or may be suspended, or

disturbed.

That it is my purpose, upon the next meeting

of Congress to again recommend the adoption of

a practical measure tendering pecuniary aid to

the free acceptance or rejection of all slave-

states, so called, the people whereof may not then

be in rebellion against the United States, and

which states, ~~and~~ ∧ may then have voluntarily adopt-

ed, or thereafter may voluntarily adopt, imme-

diate, or gradual abolishment of slavery with-

in their respective limits; and that the effort

with their consent,

to colonize persons of African descent, ∧ upon this

with the previously obtained consent of the Governments existing there,

continent, or elsewhere, ∧ will be continued.

ℐOHN HOPE FRANKLIN

The Preliminary Emancipation Proclamation of September 22, 1862, was based firmly on legislative and executive authority. As commander in chief of the army and navy, Lincoln refers to his military powers as the source of *his* authority to emancipate the slaves. This power was to be used to prosecute the war in order to restore the Union. With this document, setting the slaves free became an important means of accomplishing this end. Lincoln hoped, finally, to bring about legislative and executive cooperation with a view to developing a plan of emancipation in states that were not in rebellion. The body of the Preliminary Emancipation Proclamation is in Lincoln's own hand— with sections pasted in, and bearing fingerprints (are they his?)—and the final beginning and ending in the hand of the chief clerk. The precious document was presented by the president to the Albany Army Relief Bazaar held in February and March 1864. Gerrit Smith, the abolitionist leader, purchased it for $1,000 and gave it to the United States Sanitary Commission. Then in April 1865 the New York State Legislature appropriated $1,000 for its purchase and it was placed in the State Library—in whose possession it remains. Thank goodness for Gerrit Smith. Lincoln's handwritten copy of the final proclamation, by contrast, was lost. The president donated it to a charity fair in Chicago; there it remained, and there it later burned in the great fire. ◄

105

2

That on the first day of January in the year of
our Lord, one thousand eight hundred and sixty-
three, all persons held as slaves within any
state, or designated part of a state, the people
whereof shall then be in rebellion against the
United States shall be then, thenceforward,
and forever free; and the executive govern-
including the military and naval authority thereof
ment of the United States, will, ~~during the con~~
~~tinuance in office of the present incumbents,~~ re-
and maintain the freedom of,
cognize, such persons, ~~as being free,~~ and will
do no act or acts to repress such persons, or any
of them, in any efforts they may make for their
actual freedom.

That the executive will, on the first day of January aforesaid, by proclamation, designate the
States, and parts of states, if any, in which the
people thereof respectively, shall then be in rebellion against the United States; and the fact
that any state, or the people thereof shall, on
that day be, in good faith represented in the
Congress of the United States, by members chosen
thereto, at elections wherein a majority of the

That on the first day of January in the year of

our Lord, one thousand eight hundred and sixty-

three, all persons held as slaves within any

state, or designated part of a state, the people

whereof shall then be in rebellion against the

United States shall be then, thenceforward,

and forever free; and the executive govern-
    including the military and naval authority thereof,
ment of the United States, ∧ will during the con-

tinuance in office of the presen[?????] re-
    and maintain the freedom of
cognize ∧ such persons, as being free, and will

do no act or acts to repress such persons, or any

of them, in any efforts they may make for their

actual freedom.

That the executive will, on the first day of Jan-

uary aforesaid, by proclamation, designate the

States, and parts of states, if any, in which the

people thereof respectively, shall then be in re-

bellion against the United States; and the fact

that any state, or the people thereof shall, on

that day be, in good faith represented in the

Congress of the United States, by members chosen

thereto, at elections wherein a majority of the

PRESIDENT LINCOLN, WRITING THE PROCLAMATION OF FREEDOM,
January 1st 1863.

German-born expressionist painter David Gilmour Blythe viewed Lincoln as a liberator who drew inspiration from sacred sources—like the Bible and the Constitution—to write the Emancipation Proclamation. This print adaptation was issued in 1864 in Pittsburgh.

Another German artist—Adalbert Volck, a Confederate sympathizer in Baltimore—conversely argued that Lincoln's proclamation was inspired by sinister sources like John Brown, Satan, and alcohol.

3

qualified voters of such state shall have participa=
ted, shall, in the absence of strong countervailing
testimony, be deemed conclusive evidence that
such state and the people thereof, are not then
in rebellion against the United States.

That attention is hereby called to an Act of Congress entitled "An Act to make an additional
Article of War" approved March 13. 1862, and
which Act is in the words and figure following:

> Be it enacted by the Senate and House of Representatives of the United States of America in Congress assembled, That hereafter the following shall be promulgated as an additional article of war for the government of the army of the United States, and shall be obeyed and observed as such:
>
> Article —. All officers or persons in the military or naval service of the United States are prohibited from employing any of the forces under their respective commands for the purpose of returning fugitives from service or labor, who may have escaped from any persons to whom such service or labor is claimed to be due, and any officer who shall be found guilty by a court-martial of violating this article shall be dismissed from the service.
>
> SEC. 2. And be it further enacted, That this act shall take effect from and after its passage.

Also to the ninth and tenth sections of an
Act entitled "An Act to suppress Insurrection,
to punish Treason and Rebellion, to seize and confiscate property of rebels, and for other purposes,"
approved July 17. 1862, and which sections are
in the words and figures following:

> SEC. 9. And be it further enacted, That all slaves of persons who shall hereafter be engaged in rebellion against the government of the United States, or who shall in any way give aid or comfort thereto, escaping from such persons and taking refuge within the lines of the army; and all slaves captured from such persons or deserted by them and coming under the control of the government of the United States; and all slaves of such persons found on [or] being within any place occupied by rebel forces and afterwards occupied by the forces of the United States, shall be deemed captives of war, and shall be forever free of their servitude, and not again held as slaves.
>
> SEC. 10. And be it further enacted, That no slave escaping into any State, Territory, or the District of Columbia, from any other State, shall be delivered up, or in any way impeded or hindered of his liberty, except for crime, or some offence against the laws, unless the person claiming said fugitive shall first make oath that the person to whom the labor or service of such fugitive is alleged to be due is his lawful owner, and has not borne arms against the United States in the present rebellion, nor in any way given aid and comfort thereto; and no person engaged in the military or naval service of the United States shall, under any pretence whatever, assume to decide on the validity of the claim of any person to the service or labor of any other person, or surrender up any such person to the claimant, on pain of being dismissed from the service.

qualified voters of such state shall have participated, shall, in the absence of strong countervailing testimony, be deemed conclusive evidence that such state and the people thereof, are not then in rebellion against the United States.

That attention is hereby called to an act of Congress entitled "An act to make an additional Article of War" approved March 13, 1862, and which act is in the words and figure following:

Be it enacted by the Senate and House of Representatives of the United States of America in Congress assembled, That hereafter the following shall be promulgated as an additional article of war for the government of the army of the United States, and shall be obeyed and observed as such:

Article—. All officers or persons in the military or naval service of the United States are prohibited from employing any of the forces under their respective commands for the purpose of returning fugitives from service or labor, who may have escaped from any persons to whom such service or labor is claimed to be due, and any officer who shall be found guilty by a court-martial of violating this article shall be dismissed from the service.

SEC. 2. And be it further enacted, That this act shall take effect from and after its passage.

Also to the ninth and tenth sections of an act entitled "An Act to suppress Insurrection, to punish Treason and Rebellion, to seize and confiscate property of rebels, and for other purposes," approved July 17, 1862, and which sections are in the words and figures following:

SEC. 9. And be it further enacted, That all slaves of persons who shall hereafter be engaged in rebellion against the government of the United States, or who shall in any way give aid or comfort thereto, escaping from such persons and taking refuge within the lines of the army; and all slaves captured from such persons or deserted by them and coming under the control of the government of the United States; and all slaves of such persons found on (or) being within any place occupied by rebel forces and afterwards occupied by the forces of the United States, shall be deemed captives of war, and shall be forever free of their servitude and not again held as slaves.

SEC. 10. And be it further enacted, That no slave escaping into any State, Territory, or the District of Columbia, from any other State, shall be delivered up, or in any way impeded or hindered of his liberty, except for crime, or some offence against the laws, unless the person claiming said fugitive shall first make oath that the person to whom the labor or service of such fugitive is alleged to be due is his lawful owner, and has not borne arms against the United States in the present rebellion, nor in any way given aid and comfort thereto; and no person engaged in the military or naval service of the United States shall, under any pretence whatever, assume to decide on the validity of the claim of any person to the service or labor of any other person, or surrender up any such person to the claimant, on pain of being dismissed from the service.

PUBLISHED BY THE SUPERVISORY COMMITTEE FOR RECRUITING COLORED REGIMENTS 1210 CHESTNUT ST. PHILADELPHIA.

Lincoln's final Emancipation Proclamation added a call for black enlistment. Recruiting posters like this one showed people of color in a dignified light, a rarity until then.

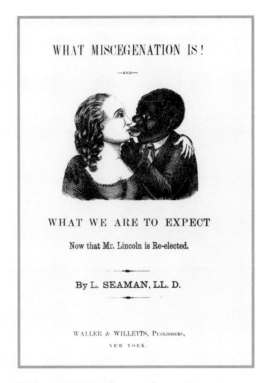

Critics warned Lincoln was a dictator intent on ushering in an era of "miscegenation"—a newly invented word for race mixing.

109

And I do hereby enjoin upon and order all persons engaged in the military and naval service of the United States to observe, obey, and enforce, within their respective spheres of service, the act, and sections above recited.

And the executive will in due time recommend that all citizens of the United States, who shall have remained loyal thereto throughout the rebellion, shall (upon the restoration of the constitutional relation between the United States, and their respective states, and people, if that relation shall have been suspended or disturbed) be compensated for all losses by acts of the United States, including the loss of slaves.

In witness whereof, I have hereunto set my hand, and caused the seal of the United States to be affixed.

L. S.

Done at the City of Washington, this twenty second day of September, in the year of our Lord, one thousand, eight hundred and sixty two, and sixty two, and of the Independence of the United States, the eighty seventh.

Abraham Lincoln.

By the President
William H. Seward,
Secretary of State

And I do hereby enjoin upon and order all persons engaged in the military and naval service of the United States to observe, obey, and enforce, within their respective spheres of service, the act, and sections above recited.

        in due time ~~at the next [????]~~

And the executive will ∧ recommend that all citizens of the United States who shall have remained loyal thereto throughout the rebellion, shall (upon the restoration of the constitutional relation between the United States, and their respective states, and people, if that relation shall have been suspended or disturbed) be compensated for all losses by acts of the United States, including the loss of slaves.

        In witness whereof, I have hereunto set my hand, and caused the seal of the United States to be affixed.

        Done at the City of Washington, this twenty second day of September,

in the year of our Lord, one thousand, eight hundred and sixty two, and sixty two and of the Independence of the United States, the eighty seventh.

        Abraham Lincoln

By the President

    William H. Seward,

        Secretary of State

However dry its intentionally legalistic language, Lincoln's society-altering final proclamation, issued January 1, 1863, inspired colorful, display-worthy renderings to decorate homes and political clubs.

Lincoln's frustration with George McClellan, his quick-to-talk and slow-to-act Union general, had many expressions. Here, perhaps, is its literary apogee, as the president's directness and concision underscore his urgency for decisive military action.

(cypher)

Executive Mansion,

Washington, May 1. 1862.

Major Gen. McClellan
Near York-Town, Va

Your call for Par-
rott guns from Washington alarms
me — chiefly because it argues
indefinite procrastination — Is
anything to be done?

A. Lincoln

Washington City. D.C.
Oct. 24. 1862

Major. Genl. McClellan

I have just read your despatch
about sore tongued and fatigued horses —
Will you pardon me for asking what the
horses of your army have done since the
battle of Antietam that fatigue anything?

A. Lincoln

JAMES M. MCPHERSON

These telegrams express Lincoln's intense and growing frustration with General George B. McClellan's endless delays and excuses for inaction in two campaigns against the enemy separated by six months and two hundred miles. In March 1862 McClellan persuaded Lincoln to approve his strategy of taking the Army of the Potomac all the way down the Potomac River and Chesapeake Bay to the tip of the Virginia peninsula at Hampton Roads for a flanking campaign against Richmond. Lincoln had instead favored direct operations against the enemy in his defensive works at Manassas only twenty-five miles from Washington, but deferred to his subordinate's supposedly superior professional military knowledge. Once McClellan arrived at Hampton Roads, the president urged him to drive quickly up the peninsula before the enemy commander, Joseph E. Johnston, could transfer his army to block McClellan's advance. "I think you better break the enemies' line from York-town to Warwick River, at once," Lincoln wired McClellan on April 6, when the Union commander had 70,000 men on this line facing only 17,000 Confederates.

Instead, McClellan settled down for a monthlong siege, calling for more big guns to blast the enemy out of his defenses. This long delay prompted Lincoln's May 1 telegram deploring the general's "indefinite procrastination."

Indefinite procrastination became McClellan's hallmark, earning him the nickname "Tardy George." Enemy commander Robert E. Lee, who took over the Army of Northern Virginia on June 1, 1862, repeatedly outwitted and outmaneuvered McClellan during the summer of 1862 and invaded Maryland in September. McClellan turned him back in the battle of Antietam on September 17, but then failed to follow up that limited victory with a vigorous pursuit despite Lincoln's pleas and orders to "destroy the rebel army, if possible." McClellan sent a steady stream of complaints and excuses to Washington, including a dispatch about fatigued and sore-tongued horses. Already stretched to the limit, Lincoln's patience snapped, and he fired back this sarcastic telegram. McClellan said that Lincoln's message made him as "mad as a 'march hare.'" It should have warned him that his tenure as commander of the Army of the Potomac would end unless he got moving. He did, but with his usual sluggishness. Two weeks later Lincoln finally removed him from command. ◄

(Cypher)

Executive Mansion,

Washington, May 1. 1862

Major Gen. McClellan

New York-Town, Va

Your call for Par-

rott guns from Washington alarms

me — chiefly because it argues

indefinite procrastination. Is

anything to be done?

A. Lincoln

Washington City, D.C.

Oct. 24. 1862

Majr. Genl. McClellan

I have just read your dispatch

about sore tongued and fatigued horses.

Will you pardon me for asking what the

horses of your army have done since the

battle of Antietam that fatigued anything?

A. Lincoln

113

The casualties of the Civil War grieved and rattled Lincoln. Yet, in his condolence letters, he captured an empathetic grace. One other gem attributed to him—the letter to Lydia Bixby—has never been found in its original form, and some scholars have questioned its authenticity. This one is unquestionably in the hand and from the mind of Lincoln.

Executive Mansion,

Washington, December 23, 1862.

Dear Fanny

It is with deep grief that I learn of the death of your Kind and brave Father; and, especially, that it is affecting your young heart beyond what is common in such cases. In this sad world of ours, sorrow comes to all; and, to the young, it comes with bitterest agony, because it takes them unawares. The older have learned to ever expect it. I am anxious to afford some alleviation of your present distress. Perfect relief is not possible, except with time. You can not now realize that you will ever feel better. Is not this so? And yet it is a mistake. You are sure to be happy again. To know this, which is certainly true, will make you some less miserable now. I have had experience enough to know what I say; and you need only to believe it, to feel better at once. The memory of your dear Father, instead of an agony, will yet be a sad sweet feeling in your heart, of a purer, and holier sort than you have known before.

Please present my kind regards to your afflicted Mother.

Your sincere friend.

Miss. Fanny McCullough.

A. Lincoln.

Executive Mansion,

Washington, December 23, 1862.

Dear Fanny

It is with deep grief that I learn of the death

of your kind and brave Father; and, especially, that it

is affecting your young heart beyond what is common in such

cases. In this sad world of ours, sorrow comes to all; and, to

the young, it comes with bitterest agony, because it takes them

unawares. The older have learned to ever expect it. I am

anxious to afford some alleviation of your present distress.

Perfect relief is not possible, except with time. You can

not now realize that you will ever feel better. Is not

this so? And yet it is a mistake. You are sure to

be happy again. To know this, which is certainly true, will

make you some less miserable now. I have had experience

enough to know what I say; and you need only to believe

it, to feel better at once. The memory of your dear Father, in-

stead of an agony, will yet be a sad sweet feeling in your

heart, of a purer, and holier sort than you have known before.

Please present my kind regards to your afflicted mother.

Your sincere friend

Miss. Fanny McCullough.   A. Lincoln.

DREW GILPIN FAUST

Often Lincoln wrote of the consolation of lives given to the nation, but here his words of sympathy are entirely personal, with no invocation of larger purposes of patriotism or sacrifice.

Lincoln was well acquainted with Lt. Colonel McCullough, an Illinois sheriff and court clerk, and had in fact interceded to gain McCullough's acceptance into the army in spite of his serious physical disabilities: partial blindness and a crippled arm. On December 5, 1862, McCullough was shot in the chest leading an assault in Coffeeville, Mississippi.

Lincoln writes to Fanny, reported to be too distressed to eat or sleep, of his own experience with grief, an experience that stretched from his mother's death when he was ten to the loss of his beloved eleven-year-old son, Willie, from typhoid just months earlier. And Lincoln felt the burden of the deaths of hundreds of thousands of men he would never know by name, men who, like McCullough, had so eagerly followed their commander in chief into war.

The Civil War brought a harvest of death to the United States, killing approximately two percent of the population of North and South, the proportional equivalent of six million men in our own time. Lincoln wrote to Fanny as the chief executive of a suffering republic, just ten days after a costly Union defeat at Fredericksburg, which yielded more than 12,000 Northern casualties.

Lincoln would spend Christmas Day visiting the sick and wounded in Washington's military hospitals. He knew more fully and compassionately than young Fanny could yet understand that "sorrow comes to all." ◄

Though hard to identify, Abraham Lincoln stands under a makeshift wooden canopy outside the U.S. Capitol as he waits to deliver his first inaugural address on March 4, 1861. Eyewitnesses testified that the crowd was the largest ever to gather for a presidential swearing-in.

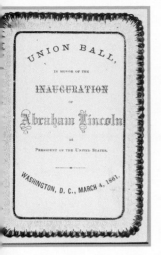

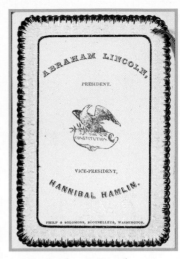

A program for the 1861 inaugural ball. Mary Lincoln entered the event on the arm of her husband's defeated opponent, Stephen A. Douglas.

[T]he Lincoln cabinet—composed of former rivals for the Republican presidential nomination who conveniently also represented different sections of the [cou]ntry, as well as varied political roots (both Whig and Democratic)—has sometimes been called the most gifted such team in presidential history. This [en]graving is based on an 1864 painting depicting the first reading of the Emancipation Proclamation.

THE FIRST READING OF THE EMANCIPATION PROCLAMATION BEFORE THE CABINET.

From the original picture painted at the White House in 1864.

Photograph by Lewis E. Walker, Washington, February 1865.

Part Four

"LET THE THING BE PRESSED"

1863-1865

― ⁊⁊⁊⁊ ―

By the final years of his life—and creative output as a writer and speaker—Lincoln firmly won not only the validation of the electorate (with a handsome reelection victory), but also the respect of America's leading authors. Even Walt Whitman and Herman Melville fell under his thrall.

This was the period of the Gettysburg Address and the Second Inaugural, two of the greatest masterpieces of American political oratory. Ironically, Lincoln initially fretted that both were failures. One friend insisted he feared Gettysburg "fell on the audience like a wet blanket." And the president initially confided of his final inaugural, "It is not immediately popular," explaining: "Men are not flattered by being shown that there has been a difference of purpose between the Almighty and them."

But Lincoln quickly came to comprehend these triumphs. The day after he returned from Gettysburg, the day's principal orator wrote to confess: "I should be glad, if I could flatter myself that I came as near to the central idea of the occasion, in two hours, as you did in two minutes." And asked to render an opinion on his 1865 inaugural, Frederick Douglass cheered: "It is a sacred effort." In four years, Lincoln's words had evolved into American scripture.

Lincoln appointed "Fighting Joe" Hooker to command the battered Army of the Potomac after the Union catastrophe at the Battle of Fredericksburg in December 1862. Hearing that his new general harbored Napoleonic delusions, the president accompanied the promotion with this extraordinary warning, tempered with words of encouragement. A few months later, Hooker led his forces into battle at Chancellorsville—and yet another defeat. Though he carried this note with him for years and thought it "beautiful…such a letter as a father might write to a son," it was not made public until 1879.

Executive Mansion,

Washington, January 26, 1863.

Major General Hooker:

General.

I have placed you at the head of the Army of the Potomac. Of course I have done this upon what appear to me to be sufficient reasons. And yet I think it best for you to know that there are some things in regard to which, I am not quite satisfied with you. I believe you to be a brave and a skilful soldier, which, of course, I like. I also believe you do not mix politics with your profession, in which you are right. You have confidence in yourself, which is a valuable, if not an indispensable quality. You are ambitious, which, within reasonable bounds, does good rather than harm. But I think that during Gen. Burnside's command of the Army, you have taken counsel of your ambition, and thwarted him as much as you could, in which you did a great wrong to the country, and to a most meritorious and honorable brother officer. I have heard, in such way as to believe it, of your recent

GABOR BORITT

Executive Mansion,

Washington, January 26, 1863.

Major General Hooker:

General,

I have placed you at the head of the Army of the Potomac. Of course I have done this upon what appears to me to be sufficient reasons. And yet I think it is best for you to know that there are some things in regard to which, I am not quite satisfied with you. I believe you to be a brave and a skilful soldier, which, of course, I like. I also believe you do not mix politics with your profession, in which you are right. You have confidence in yourself, which is a valuable, if not an indispensable quality. You are ambitious, which, within reasonable bounds, does good rather than harm. But I think that during Gen. Burnside's command of the Army, you have taken counsel of your ambition, and thwarted him as much as you could, in which you did a great wrong to the country, and to a most meritorious and honorable brother officer. I have heard, in such way as to believe it, of your recent-

What? A dictatorship? In the United States? This idea seems unbelievable today. A commander in chief is in control of military as well as civil leadership. This is a given.

But it had not been a given in much of humanity over the history of time. The United States tried to create a better world at the end of the eighteenth century. Then the American Civil War produced new problems. By 1863 many Americans thought their government had been defeated. Among others, one of the most popular Union generals, "Fighting Joe" Hooker, announced that the government was "imbecile." What the people needed was a "dictator, and the sooner the better." Some people took the general's comments seriously, as did others before. Though Lincoln believed Hooker to be a hothead, the president also believed that the general was the best man for the time. Lincoln appointed him. At the same time, he also wrote one of his most blunt personal letters to Hooker. The president understood that some generals needed to grow up. ◄

by saying that both the Army, and the Government needed a Dictator. Of course it was not for this, but in spite of it, that I have given you the command. Only those generals who gain successes, can set up dictators. What I now ask of you is military success, and I will risk the dictatorship. The government will support you to the utmost of its ability, which is neither more nor less than it has done and will do for all commanders. I much fear that the spirit which you have aided to infuse into the Army, of criticising their Commanders, and withholding confidence from him, will now turn upon you. I shall assist you as far as I can, to put it down. Neither you, nor Napoleon, if he were alive again, could get any good out of an army, while such a spirit prevails in it.

And now, beware of rashness— Beware of rashness, but with energy, and sleepless vigilance, go forward, and give us victories.

Yours very truly,

A. Lincoln

ly saying that both the Army and the Government needed a Dictator. Of course it was not <u>for</u> this, but in spite of it, that I have given you the command. Only those generals who gain successes, can set up dictators. What I now ask of you is military success, and I will risk the dictatorship. The government will support you to the utmost of it's ability, which is neither more nor less than it has done and will do for all commanders. I much fear that the spirit which you have aided to infuse into the Army, of criticizing their commander, and withholding confidence from him, will now turn upon you. I shall assist you as far as I can, to put it down. Neither you, nor Napoleon, if he were could alive again, ~~can~~ get any good out of an army, while such a spirit prevails in it.

   And now, beware of rashness. Beware of rashness, but with energy, and sleepless vigilance, go forward, and give us victories.

Yours very truly

A. Lincoln

Lincoln and General Hooker (to his left, his head later cut from the picture) review the Army of the Potomac at its encampment near Falmouth, Virginia, in April 1863. One soldier thought the tall visitor, his long legs practically scraping the ground, "presented a very comical picture." But in the words of another eyewitness, "that sad anxious face, so full of melancholy foreboding," made ridicule impossible.

President Lincoln was a fixture at the telegraph office in Washington, where the latest technology kept him engaged with his generals in the field. On the morning of June 9, he had another kind of urgent message—to his wife, about his ten-year-old son, Thomas "Tad" Lincoln.

Thomas Mallon

Executive Mansion,

Washington, June 9, 1863.

Mrs. Lincoln

    Philadelphia, Pa.

    Think you better put "Tad's" pistol away. I had an ugly dream about him.

    A. Lincoln

As his worried father knew, Tad Lincoln loved uniforms, swords, and guns. The youngster not only posed for this photograph wearing a custom-made soldier's suit and toting a miniature rifle; he elaborated on it by inking in a manly goatee. His parents kept the comical result in their family album.

Lincoln paid serious attention to the portents his dreams might be carrying. After the death of his son Willie, he was even more likely to ponder any nightmare involving harm to (or done by?) Tad, his elfin, rambunctious, and overindulged ten-year-old. Whatever the precise nature of Lincoln's dream about the pistol, its urgency prompted the president to compose this note for the operator of the military telegraph, who dispatched its gentle suggestion to the First Lady while she traveled with Tad in Philadelphia.

How odd that this boy, thus protected from his own pistol, should two years later assist in the giving of a speech that hastened his father's death by John Wilkes Booth's derringer. Three nights before the assassination, Tad accompanied Lincoln to an open window of the White House, from which the president delivered remarks envisioning suffrage for a portion of the freed slaves. "Now, by God, I'll put him through," declared Booth, standing with one of his co-conspirators among the listeners. As Lincoln finished reading the loose pages of his text, he allowed each one to fall from his hand. Tad made a game of catching them before they could hit the ground. ◄

Lincoln wrote the long letter from which this section is excerpted in reply to angry resolutions from
New York Democrats in Albany, who condemned his suspension of the writ of habeas corpus.
Widely published, the reply proved a tactical victory for Lincoln, though debate over a president's
constitutional authority in wartime has never ended. *(Excerpt)*

13

Take the particular case mentioned by the meeting. They
in substance
assert, that Mr. Vallandigham was, seized and tried by a military commander.
"for no other reason than words, addressed to a public
meeting, in criticism of the course of the administration,
and in condemnation of the military orders of
that general" Now, if there be no mistake about this—
if this assertion is the truth and the whole truth—
if there was no other reason for the arrest, then I concede that the arrest was wrong. But the arrest, as
I understand, was made for a very different reason. Mr. Vallandigham avows his hostility to the war
on the part of the Union; and his arrest was made
because he was laboring, with some effect, to prevent
the raising of troops, to encourage desertions from the army, and to leave the rebellion without an adequate
military force to suppress it. He was not arrested because he was damaging the political prospects of the administration, or the personal interests of the commanding
general; but because he was damaging the army, upon
the existence, and vigor of which, the life of the nation
depends. He was warring upon the military; and this
gave the military constitutional jurisdiction to lay

Take the particular case mentioned by the meeting. They
    in substance   by a military commander,
assert ∧ that Mr. Vallandigham was ∧ seized and tried

"for no other reason than words addressed to a public

meeting, in criticism of the course of the administration,

and in condemnation of the military orders of

that general" Now, if there be no mistake about this —

if this assertion is the truth and the whole truth —

if there was no other reason for the arrest, then I con-

cede that the arrest was wrong. But the arrest, as

I understand, was made for a very different reas-

on. Mr. Vallandigham avows his hostility to the war

on the part of the Union; and his arrest was made

because he was laboring, with some effect, to prevent

the raising of troops, to encourage desertions from the ar-

my, and to leave the rebellion without an adequate

military force to suppress it. He was not arrested be-

cause he was damaging the political prospects of the ad-

ministration, or the personal interests of the commanding

general; but because he was damaging the army, upon

the existence, and vigor of which, the life of the nation

depends. He was warring upon the military; and this

gave the military constitutional jurisdiction to lay

DAVID HERBERT DONALD

The task of shaping public opinion was not easy, and Lincoln's view of the proprieties of his office did not make it easier. He followed his predecessors in refraining from making public addresses while in the White House. "In my present position," he told a crowd in 1862, eager to hear his plans and hopes, "it is hardly proper for me to make speeches." But in a series of magnificent public letters, which were carried in nearly every important newspaper in the country, he made it clear that he had become not merely a president who presided over the usual transactions of government, but a transforming leader who was changing the very nature of discourse about the war. In this letter, written in June 1863, in reply to the protests of New York Democratic politicians over the suspension of habeas corpus and, in particular, over the arrest of Congressman Clement L. Vallandigham for inciting resistance to the draft, he offers a carefully reasoned defense of his decision to invoke the war power to act for the public good. Then he asks, in language that any reader could understand: "Must I shoot a simple-minded soldier boy who deserts, while I must not touch the hair of a wiley agitator who induces him to desert?" Thus in twenty-five words Lincoln summarized one of the most difficult problems the leader of a democratic society must face: how to reconcile liberty and order. ◄

14

hands upon him. If Mr. Vallandigham was not dam=
aging the military power of the country, then his arrest
was made on mistake of fact, which I would be glad
to correct, on reasonably satisfactory evidence.

I understand the meeting, whose resolutions I am consid=
ering, to be in favor of suppressing the rebellion by mili=
tary force— by armies. Long experience has shown that ar=
mies can not be maintained unless desertion shall
be punished by the severe penalty of death. The case
requires, and the law and the constitution, sanction this pun=
ishment— Must I shoot a simple-minded soldier boy
who deserts, while I must not touch a hair of a wi=
                        This is none the less injurious when effected by
ley agitator who induces him to desert;— by getting a
father, or brother, or friend, into a public meeting,
and there working upon his feelings, till he is per=
suaded to write the soldier boy, that he is fighting in
a bad cause, for a wicked administration of a contempt=
able government, too weak to arrest and punish him if
he shall desert. I think that in such a case, to
silence the agitator, and save the boy, is not only con=
stitutional, but, withal, a great mercy.

                    question of Constitutional power,
If I be wrong on this, my error lies in believing

hands upon him. If Mr. Vallandigham was not dam-

aging the military power of the country, then his arrest

was made on mistake of fact, which I would be glad
to correct, on reasonably satisfactory evidence.
I understand the meeting, whose resolutions I am consid-

ering, to be in favor of suppressing the rebellion by mili-

tary force — by armies. Long experience has shown that ar-

mies can not be maintained unless desertion shall

be punished by the severe penalty of death. The case

requires, and the law and the constitution, sanction this pun-

ishment. Must I shoot a simple-minded soldier boy

who deserts, while I must not touch a hair of a wi-
       This is none the less injurious when effected by
ley agitator who induces him to desert? ~~by~~ ∧ getting ~~his~~ a

father, or brother, or friend, into a public meeting,

and there working upon his feelings, till he is per-

suaded to write the soldier boy, that he is fighting in

a bad cause, for a wicked administration of a contempt-

able government, too weak to arrest and punish him if

he shall desert. I think that in such a case, to

silence the agitator, and save the boy, is not only con-

stitutional, but, withal, a great mercy. ~~and a great mer-~~

~~it.~~
          question of Constitutional power,
If I be wrong on this subject, ∧ ~~subject~~, my error lies in believing

Clement Laird Vallandigham, the antiwar
Ohio politician whose arrest, military trial
for treason, and banishment to the
Confederacy inspired Albany Democrats to
rebuke Lincoln—in turn provoked the
president's response to Erastus Corning.

The great American WHAT IS IT? chased by Copperheads

A bedraggled Lincoln defiantly shreds the Constitution as he flees from
"Copperhead" snakes out to avenge Vallandigham. In the background,
one of the reptiles chokes General Ambrose Burnside, who had ordered
"Valiant Val's" seizure. This cartoon was copyrighted just two weeks
after Lincoln issued his letter to Corning.

"The Tycoon is in very good humor," White House secretary John Hay wrote in his diary on July 19, 1863. That day, a jubilant Lincoln scribbled this irreverent verse to mark the recent Union triumph at Gettysburg. Lost for nearly a century, it was rediscovered in Hay's papers in the 1960s.

Gen. Lees invasion of the North, written by himself—

"In eighteen sixty three, with pomp,
          and mighty swell,
The mad Jeff's Confederacy, went
          forth to sack Phil-del,
The Yankees, they got arter us, and
          giv us particular hell,
And we skedaddled back again,
          and didn't sack Phil-del.

Written Sunday morning July 19. 1863.

Attest John Hay.

NEWT GINGRICH

Gen. Lees invasion of the

North, written by himself.

"In eighteen sixty three, with pomp,

and mighty swell,

Me and Jeff's Confederacy, went

forth to sack Phil-del.

The Yankees they got arter us, and

giv us particlar hell,

And we skedaddled back again,

and didn't sack Phil-del.

Written Sunday morning July 19. 1863.

attest John Hay.

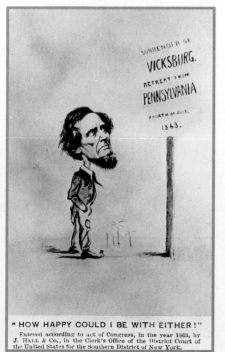

" HOW HAPPY COULD I BE WITH EITHER !"
Entered according to act of Congress, in the year 1863, by
J. HALL & Co., in the Clerk's Office of the District Court of
the United States for the Southern District of New York.

Lincoln's doggerel about Lee's defeat at Gettysburg and retreat from Pennsylvania is characteristic of Lincoln's passion for humor and use of poetry. Lincoln routinely opened his cabinet meetings with humor. All his life he had used humor to entertain people on the court circuit as a lawyer and as a campaigner.

Lincoln collected humorous stories, read most of the famous humorists of his time (their version of *The Tonight Show* as a weekly column), and gathered funny stories and funny insights.

From the time he studied the Bible and Shakespeare, Lincoln became fascinated with words and how they could be strung together to evoke images, emotions, and insights.

Lincoln is the greatest wordsmith to have occupied the White House. That ability came from a constant fascination with language and a constant playing with ideas. He collected scraps of paper on which he wrote different thoughts and insights. His Second Inaugural Address in March 1865 grew out of notes made in August 1862.

These patterns of humor, poetry, wordsmithery, and constant thought come together in this expression of glee that Lee's audacious gamble had been defeated and the seemingly ever-victorious Army of Northern Virginia had been proven capable of defeat.

Combined with the victory at Vicksburg the same week, Lincoln suddenly had a lot to be excited and happy about. A humorous doggerel was a good device for him to let some of that joy out without risking public exposure. ◄

As further evidence of Lincoln's jolly mood after the Union triumph at Gettysburg, he owned this *carte-de-visite* cartoon showing Jefferson Davis pondering his ruination.

In despair over Meade's failure to pursue Robert E. Lee's army as it retreated south from Gettysburg, Lincoln vented his anger with this rebuke—tempered with praise for the recent Union victory—then thought better of it. The letter was "never sent, or signed."

Executive Mansion,

Washington, July 14 , 1863.

Major General Meade

I have just seen your despatch to Gen. Halleck, asking to be relieved of your command, because of a supposed censure of mine. I am very—*very*—grateful to you for the magnificient success you gave the cause of the country at Gettysburg; and I am sorry now to be the author of the slightest pain to you— But I was in such deep distress myself that I could not restrain some expression of it— I have been oppressed nearly ever since the battles at Gettysburg, by what appeared to be evidences that yourself, and Gen. Couch, and Gen. Smith, were not seeking a collision with the enemy, but were trying to get him across the river without another battle. What these evidences were, if you please, I hope to tell you at some time, when we shall both feel better. The case, summarily stated is this. You fought and beat the enemy at Gettysburg; and, of course, to say the least, his loss was as great as yours— He retreated; and you did not, as it seemed to me, pressingly pursue him; but a flood in the river detained him, till, by slow degrees, you were again upon him. You had at least twenty thous-

Executive Mansion,

Washington, July 14, 1863.

Major General Meade

I have just seen your despatch to
Gen. Halleck, asking to be relieved of your command, because of a supposed censure of mine. I
am very — <u>very</u> — grateful to you for the magnificient
success you gave the cause of the country at Gettys
burg; and I am sorry now to be _∧ the author of the slightest
pain to you. But I was in such deep distress my-
self that I could not restrain some expression of
it. I had been oppressed nearly ever since the battles
at Gettysburg, by what appeared to be evidences that your
self, and Gen. Couch, and Gen. Smith, were not seeking a collision with the enemy, but were trying to get
him across the river without another battle. What these
evidences were, if you please, I hope to tell you at some
time, when we shall both feel better. The case, summarily stated is this. You fought and beat the enemy
at Gettysburg; and, of course, to say the least, his loss
was as great as yours. He retreated; and you did not,
as it seemed to me, pressingly pursue him; but a flood
in the river detained him, till, by slow degrees, you
were again upon him. You had at least twenty thous-

Lincoln's turbulent emotional depths and his
bracingly unencumbered rationality form one
of the paradoxes that make him inexhaustibly
interesting. Both are present in the Meade
letter, which offers a privileged glimpse into
the way these coexisted in his complicated
soul.

The lucidity of the letter is characteristic
of the president's close attention to the
conduct of the war, his coolly precise tactical
understanding, informed and finely detailed.
It's the clarity that William Herndon, his law
partner, called Lincoln's "perfect mental lens."
The heat of his exasperation is felt ("And
Couch and Smith!") but Lincoln's analysis of
Meade's errors is undistorted by that heat,
delivered in concise, flourish-free prose that's
all the more blistering for what's implicit in its
restraint. There were no words to elaborate
upon "the magnitude of the misfortune." It
was so overwhelming as to be unsayable.
Reverend Henry Fowler wrote that Lincoln's
style was "oftentimes of Saxon force and
classic purity." The sentence "As it is, the war
will go on indefinitely" has, in its
compression, some of the same power as the
devastating four words Lincoln spoke twenty
months later, at his second inaugural: "And the
war came."

But the most remarkable line of the
Meade letter, and in a sense its most
Lincolnian feature, is the faint note written
(by what to our eyes seems a hand other than
Lincoln's) on the last page. "President's
endorsement on the envelope: To Gen. Meade,
never sent or signed."

(continued)

133

and veteran troops directly with you, and as many
more raw ones within supporting distance, all in addition to those who fought with you at Gettysburg;
while it was not possible that he had received a
single recruit; and yet you stood and let the
flood run down, bridges be built, and then move
move away at his leisure, without attacking him.
And Couch and Smith! The latter left Carlisle in time,
upon all ordinary calculation, to have aided you in the
last battle at Gettysburg; but he did not arrive. At the end of now
then ten days, I believe twelve, under constant urging,
he reached Hagerstown from Carlisle, which is not
an inch over fiftyfive miles, if so much. And Couch's
movement was very little different.

Again, my dear general, I do not believe you appreciate the magnitude of the misfortune involved in Lee's escape. He was within your very grasp, and to have
closed upon him would, in connection with the our
other late successes, have ended the war. As it is,
the war will be prolonged indefinitely. If you could
not safely attack Lee last monday, how can you
possibly do so South of the river, when you can take
with you very few more than two thirds of the force
you then had in hand? It would be unreasonable

134

and veteran troops directly with you, and as many more raw ones within supporting distance, all in addition to those who fought with you at Gettysburg; while it was not possible that he had received a single recruit; and yet you stood and let the flood run down, bridges be built, and the enemy move away at his leisure, without attacking him.

And Couch and Smith! The latter left Carlisle in time, upon all ordinary calculation, to have aided you in the last battle at Gettysburg; but he did not arrive. ~~More~~ At the end of more than ten days, I believe twelve, under constant urging, he reached Hagerstown from Carlisle, which is not an inch over fiftyfive miles, if so much. And Couch's movement was very little different.

Again, my dear general, I do not believe you appreciate the magnitude of the misfortune involved in Lee's escape. He was within your easy grasp, and to have closed upon him would, in connection with ~~the~~ our other late successes, have ended the war. As it is, the war will be prolonged indefinitely. If you could not safely attack Lee last monday, how can you possibly do so South of the river, when you can take with you very few more than two thirds of the force you then had in hand? It would be unreasonable

Though it was occasioned by Meade's request to be relieved of command, this is neither an official admonishment nor an official refusal of the request (Lincoln is always cagey). Its incisiveness notwithstanding, the letter began as a personal communication from one anguished man to another. Emotional agony, sorrow, reluctance, "magnificent success" and "deep distress," gratitude, affection, regret, and painful anger are arrayed in uncomfortable proximity, with no attempt by the writer to reconcile conflict.

The impulse to blame, as rare in Lincoln as self-pity, originates in memory, in the past. The past mattered to Lincoln; his contention that slavery and inequality were inimical to democracy and union was built on antecedence, on a study of legal and legislative history. But as his evolving ideas for reconstruction showed, judging people for what they'd done was far less meaningful to Lincoln than holding people to declarations of what they intended to do. The past had to be confronted for the purpose of being released from it, so that the future would become conceivable.

(continued)

General George G. Meade led Union troops to victory at Gettysburg after less than a week in command of the army, but aroused Lincoln's wrath anyway for failing to pursue Lee's Confederates.

to expect, and I do not expect you can now effect
much. Your golden opportunity is gone, and I am distressed immeasurably because of it.

I beg you will not consider this a prosecution, or persecution of yourself. As you had learned that I was
dissatisfied, I have thought it best to kindly tell you
why.

President's endorsement on the envelope:
    "To Gen. Meade, never sent or signed."

to expect, and I do not expect you can now effect much. Your golden opportunity is gone, and I am distressed immeasureably because of it.

I beg you will not consider this a prossecution, or persecution of yourself. As you had learned that I was dissatisfied, I have thought it best to kindly tell you why.

President's endorsement on the envelope:

"To Gen. Meade, never sent, or signed."

That the letter would never be sent is perhaps foreshadowed by Lincoln's anticipation of further discussion with Meade at a time "when we shall both feel better." What Lincoln began as correspondence on July 14 became contemplative, an introspective working through of rage and despair that results in an emancipation of empathy. Meade would never be officially reprimanded for Lee's escape at Gettysburg, nor would he be exculpated by the president. It's not clear that he should have been entirely forgiven, though Lincoln eventually doubted whether Meade, new to his command of the Army of the Potomac, could have asked more of his exhausted men after their epic struggle. There's a short speech, delivered four months later at Gettysburg, that gives a fair account of what Lincoln came to believe was accomplished there.

In 1861, Secretary of State William Seward observed to his wife, Frances, that Lincoln's "confidence and sympathy increase almost every day." Since a prevalent assumption of the politics of our own time has been that confidence and sympathy are antagonistic qualities, that compassion weakens authority and strength is a betrayal of kindness, it's worth considering the combination of attributes Seward discerned in his beleaguered president. ◄

LETTERS TO **JAMES HACKETT**, AUGUST 17, 1863 AND NOVEMBER 2, 1863
Lincoln's audacious but heartfelt comments on Shakespeare were leaked to the press
by their recipient, actor James Hackett, and much mocked.

Executive Mansion,

Washington, August 17 . 1863.

My dear Sir:

Months ago I should have acknowledged the
receipt of your book, and accompanying kind note; and
I now have to beg your pardon for not having done so.

For one of my age, I have seen very little of the drama.
The first presentation of Falstaff I ever saw was yours here,
last winter or spring. Perhaps the best compliment I can
pay is to say, as I truly can, I am very anxious to see
it again. Some of Shakspeare's plays I have never read;
while others I have gone over perhaps as frequently as any
unprofessional reader. Among the latter are Lear, Richard Third, Henry Eighth, Hamlet, and especially Macbeth. I think nothing equals Macbeth. It is wonderful.
Unlike you gentlemen of the profession, I think the soliloquy
in Hamlet commencing "O, my offense is rank" surpasses
that commencing "To be, or not to be." But pardon this small
attempt at criticism. I should like to hear you pronounce
the opening speech of Richard the Third. Will you not
soon visit Washington again? If you do, please call and
let me make your personal acquaintance.

Yours truly

James H. Hackett, Esq.   A. Lincoln.

Executive Mansion,

Washington, August 17, 1863.

My dear Sir:

Months ago I should have acknowledged the receipt of your book, and accompanying kind note; and I now have to beg your pardon for not having done so.

For one of my age, I have seen very little of the drama. The first presentation of Falstaff I ever saw was yours here, last winter or spring. Perhaps the best compliment I can pay is to say, as I truly can, I am very anxious to see it again. Some of Shakspeare's plays I have never read; while others I have gone over perhaps as frequently as any unprofessional reader. Among the latter are Lear, Richard Third, Henry Eighth, Hamlet, and especially Macbeth. I think nothing equals Macbeth. It is wonderful. Unlike you gentlemen of the profession, I think the soliloquy in Hamlet commencing "O, my offence is rank" surpasses that commencing "To be, or not to be." But pardon this small attempt at criticism. I should like to hear you pronounce the opening speech of Richard the Third. Will you not soon visit Washington again? If you do, please call and let me make your personal acquaintance.

Yours truly

James H. Hackett, Esq.   A. Lincoln.

ℒIAM NEESON

Many thoughts struck me as I read Lincoln's letters to actor James Hackett, not least that he was feeling relaxed enough to answer nonurgent mail! The decisive Gettysburg victory, followed by the surrender of Vicksburg the following day on the Fourth of July (which General Lee later admitted was the decisive event of the war), must have, finally, warmed the heart of the president and made him feel that victory was, perhaps, within sight—that this "great trouble" might soon be over.

Lincoln fell in love with the works of Shakespeare as a young man and that love became stronger during his years in office, as Shakespeare's insights into the human condition and the substance of his plays gave solace to Lincoln's deepening sense of tragedy as the Civil War progressed.

Watching Hackett's performance of Falstaff in *Henry IV* (to which the first letter refers), the president was seen to be sad but very focused on what was being said onstage, as if to ascertain the correctness of his own conception as compared with that of the professional artist.

I find it interesting that Lincoln says, "I think nothing equals *Macbeth*." Here is a play about power, politics, jealousy, treason, and planning war campaigns, all of which he is dealing with as president—while, like Macbeth, married to a woman who is as ambitious as he is and gradually growing more paranoid. Perhaps Lincoln felt he too had blood on his hands from the continuing carnage.

(continued)

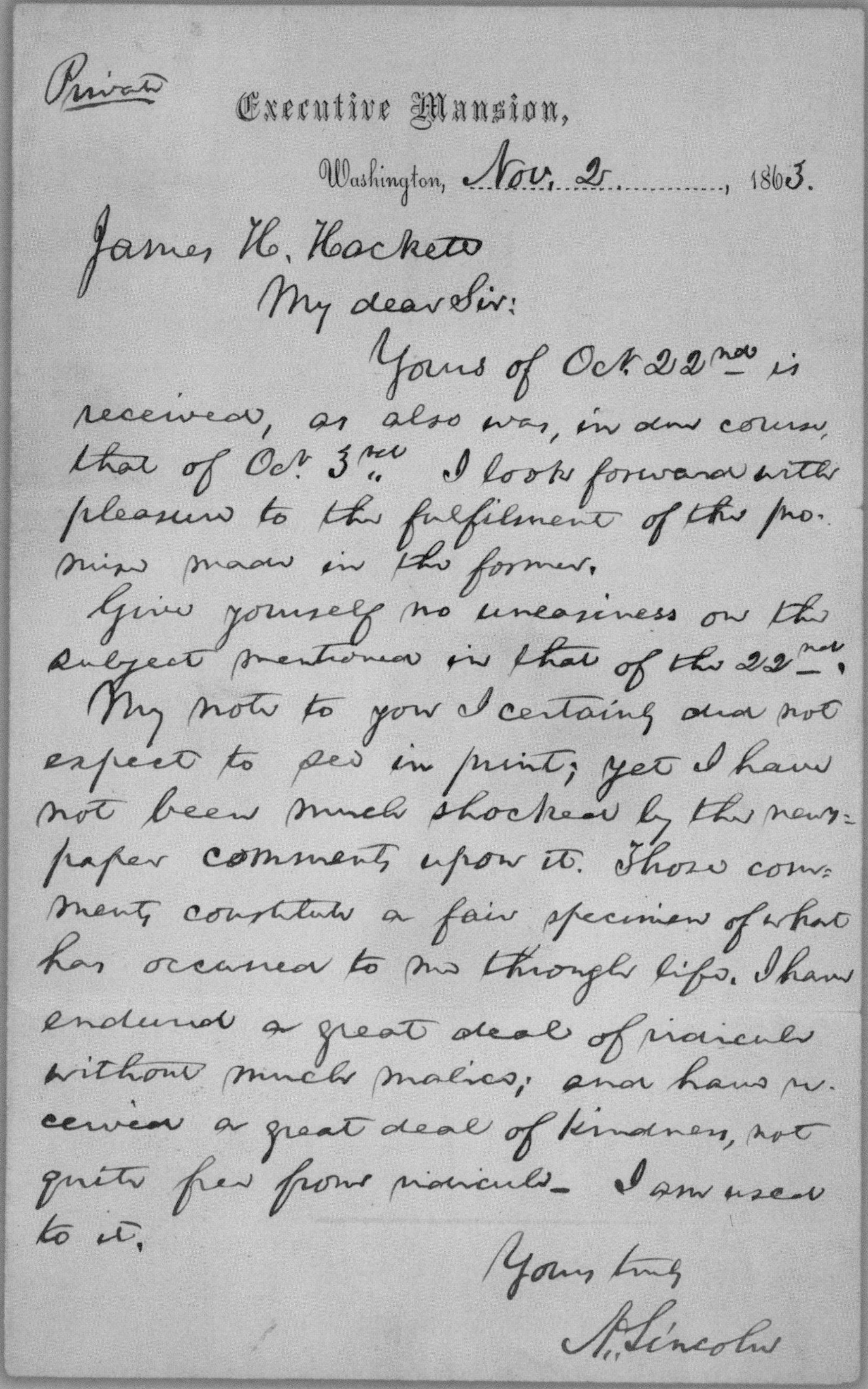

Private

Executive Mansion,

Washington, *Nov. 2*, 186*3*.

James H. Hackett

    My dear Sir:

       Yours of Oct 22ⁿᵈ is received, as also was, in due course, that of Oct 3ʳᵈ. I look forward with pleasure to the fulfilment of the promise made in the former.

    Give yourself no uneasiness on the subject mentioned in that of the 22ⁿᵈ.

    My note to you I certainly did not expect to see in print; yet I have not been much shocked by the newspaper comments upon it. Those comments constitute a fair specimen of what has occurred to me through life. I have endured a great deal of ridicule without much malice; and have received a great deal of kindness, not quite free from ridicule. I am used to it.

           Yours truly

           A. Lincoln

Executive Mansion,

Washington, Nov. 2, 1863.

James H. Hackett

My dear Sir:

Yours of Oct. 22nd is

received, as also was, in due course,

that of Oct. 3rd I look forward with

pleasure to the fulfillment of the pro-

mise made in the former.

Give yourself no uneasiness on the

subject mentioned in that of the 22nd.

My note to you I certainly did not

expect to see in print; yet I have

not been much shocked by the news-

paper comments upon it. Those com-

ments constitute a fair specimen of what

has occurred to me through life. I have

endured a great deal of ridicule

without much malice; and have re-

ceived a great deal of kindness, not

quite free from ridicule. I am used

to it.

Yours truly,

A. Lincoln

Then he picks Claudius's soliloquy from *Hamlet*, act three, scene three, as a particular favorite. This is a character asking himself if he can ever be forgiven for his heinous crime. (He killed his brother, Hamlet's father.) And though he prays, his prayers have no value ("my words fly up, my thoughts remain below"). One can only imagine the long, lonely days and nights where Lincoln must have confronted his id, analyzed the nature of the war and its consequences and, indeed, tried to offer up prayers for, perhaps, forgiveness and blessed release.

I do agree with the great Walt Whitman, who, in comparing President Lincoln to Shakespeare, said: "What Shakespeare did in poetic expression, Abraham Lincoln essentially did in his personal and official life." The sixteenth president of the United States was a pretty good poet as well and, boy, could he write a letter! No wonder Hackett had it printed and distributed to all his "friends"! ◄

A period theatrical poster showing actor James Hackett in his signature role. Lincoln once termed the rebellion "these days of villainy," pointing out: "it is old 'Jack Falstaff' who talks about 'villainy,' though of course Shakespeare is responsible."

An invitation to a pro-Union rally inspired this extraordinary defense of emancipation
and black enlistment. Lincoln wrote the letter as an oration to be read aloud
by a surrogate, whom he instructed to speak "very slowly"—
the way Lincoln himself delivered speeches.

1

Executive Mansion,

Washington, August 26, 1863.

Hon. James C. Conkling

My dear Sir:

Your letter inviting me to attend
a mass-meeting of unconditional Union-men, to be
held at the Capital of Illinois, on the 3rd day of
September, has been received. It would be very agreeable to me, to thus meet my old friends, at my own
home; but I can not, just now, be absent from
here, so long as a visit there, would require.

The meeting is to be of all those who maintain unconditional devotion to the Union; and I am sure my old political
friends will thank me for tendering, as I do, the nation's
gratitude to those other noble men, whom no partizan
malice, or partizan hope, can make false to the nation's life—

Executive Mansion,

Washington, August 26, 1863.

Hon. James C. Conkling

My dear Sir:

Your letter inviting me to attend

a mass-meeting of unconditional Union-men, to be

held at the Capital of Illinois, on the 3rd day of

September, has been received. It would be very agree-

able to me, to thus meet my old friends, at my own

home; but I can not, just now, be absent from

here, so long as a visit there, would require.

The meeting is to be of all those who maintain uncondi-

tional devotion to the union; and I am sure my old political
∧ friends will thank me for tendering, as I do, the nation's

gratitude to those other noble men, whom no partizan

malice, or partizan hope, can make false to the na-

tion's life.

PRESIDENT BILL CLINTON

In the midst of the Civil War, President Lincoln was invited to a meeting in his hometown of Springfield, Illinois, to address Union supporters, including some who were opposed to the Emancipation Proclamation, which they believed made it more difficult to negotiate an end to the war.

Lincoln couldn't attend the meeting, but sent this remarkable letter to be read in his absence. After thanking those in attendance for supporting the Union, Lincoln takes on his critics in trademark fashion, stating their arguments, then demolishing them. He defends his authority to emancipate the slaves and denies the possibility of any acceptable negotiated end to the war. He entreats them to embrace victory as the only practical alternative, even if they reject the moral ground on which he stands. "You say you will not fight to free negroes. Some of them seem willing to fight for you; but, no matter. Fight you, then, exclusively to save the Union."

Just as they did in 1863, Lincoln's words ring strong and true today, another time of complex challenges and elusive solutions. We can learn a lot from Lincoln's constant search for the right mix of persuasion and power, mind and heart, to preserve and perfect our Union. ◄

There are those who are dissatisfied with me. To such I would say: You desire peace, and you blame me that we do not have it. But how can we attain it? There are but three conceivable ways. First, to suppress the rebellion by force of arms. This I am trying to do. Are you for it? If you are, so far we are agreed— If you are not for it, a second way is to give up the Union— I am against this— Are you for it? If you are, you should say so plainly— If you are not for force, nor yet for dissolution, there only remains some immaginable compromise. I do not believe any compromise, embracing the maintainance of the Union, is now possible. All I learn leads to a directly opposite belief— The strength of the rebellion, is its military— its army— That army dominates all the country, and all the people, within its range. Any offer of terms made by any man or men within that range, in opposition to that army, is simply nothing for the present; because such man or men, have no power whatever to enforce their side of a compromise, if one were made with them. To illustrate. Suppose refugees from the South, and peace men of the North, get together in convention, and frame and proclaim a compromise embracing a restoration of the Union, in what way can that compromise be used to keep Lee's army out of Pennsylvania? Meade's army can keep Lee's army out of Pennsylvania; and, I think, can ultimately drive

There are those who are dissatisfied with me. To such I would say: You desire peace; and you blame me that we do not have it. But how can we attain it? There are but three conceivable ways. First, to suppress the rebellion by force of arms. This I am trying to do. Are you for it? If you are, so far we are agreed. If you are not for it, a second way is to give up the Union. I am against this. Are you for it? If you are, you should say so plainly. If you are not for <u>force</u>, nor yet for dissolution, there only remains some immaginable <u>compromise</u>. I do not believe any compromise, embracing the maintainance of the union, is now possible. All I learn leads to a directly opposite belief. The strength of the rebellion, is it's military — it's army. That army dominates all the country, and all the people, within it's range. Any offer of terms made by any man or men within that range, in opposition to that army, is simply nothing for the present; because such man or men, have no power whatever to enforce their side of a compromise, if one were made with them. To illustrate. Suppose refugees from the South, and peace men of the North, get together in convention, and frame and proclaim a compromise embracing a restoration of the Union, in what way can that compromise be used to keep Lee's army out of Pennsylvania? Meade's army can keep Lees army out of Pennsylvania; and, I think, can ultimately drive

While some Northerners doubted—and many Southerners feared—the Union plan to arm its newly recruited African-American troops, this *Harper's Weekly* cover illustration, published in March 1863, made the case that the new troops would make fine soldiers. Such images served to reassure nervous whites.

3

it out of existence. But no paper compromise to which the
controllers of Lee's army are not agreed, can at all affect
that army. In an effort at such compromise we should
waste time, which the enemy would improve to our disadvantage; and that would be all. A compromise, to be effective, must be made, either with those who control the
rebel army, or with the people first liberated from the
domination of that army, by the successes of our own army.
Now allow me to assure you, that no word or intimation, from that rebel army, or from any of the men controlling
it, in relation to any peace compromise, has ever come to my
knowledge, ~~information~~ or belief. All charges and insinua-
tions to the contrary, are deceptive, and groundless. ~~utterly, and offensively false~~

And I promise you that if any such proposition shall
hereafter come, it shall not be rejected, and kept
a secret from you. I freely acknowledge myself the
servant of the people, according to the bond of service-
the United States Constitution; and that, as such, I am
responsible to them.

But, to be plain, you are dissatisfied with me about
the negro. Quite likely there is a difference of opinion between you and myself upon that subject. I certainly wish that all men could be free, while I
suppose you do not. Yet I have neither adopted

it out of existence. But no paper compromise to which the controllers of Lee's army are not agreed, can at all affect that army. In an effort at such compromise we should waste time, which the enemy would improve to our disadvantage; and that would be all. A compromise, to be effective, must be made, either with those who control the rebel army, or with the people first liberated from the domination of that army, by the successes of our own army. Now allow me to assure you, that no word or intimation, from the rebel army, or from any of the men controlling it, in relation to any peace compromise, has ever come to my knowledge, ~~information~~ or belief. All charges and insinuations to the contrary, are ~~utter humbuggery and falsehood~~ deceptive, and groundless.

And I promise you that if any such proposition shall hereafter come, it shall not be rejected, and kept a secret from you. I freely acknowledge myself the servant of the people, according to the bond of service — the United States constitution; and that, as such, I am responsible to them.

But, to be plain, you are dissatisfied with me about the negro. Quite likely there is a difference of opinion between you and myself upon that subject. I certainly wish that all men could be free, while I suppose you do not. Yet I have neither adopted

Lincoln entrusted James C. Conkling, his longtime intimate from Springfield, to deliver a crucial public letter. It helped that Lincoln considered Conkling "one of the best public readers."

A row of modern buildings rises over the public square in Lincoln's once-sleepy Springfield hometown—now a thriving city—where his Conkling "letter" was delivered in 1863.

4

Executive Mansion,

Washington, _____ , 186 .

nor proposed any measure, which is not consistent with even your view, provided you are for the Union— I suggested compensated emancipation; to which you replied you wished not to be taxed to buy negroes. But I have not asked you to be taxed to buy negroes, except in such way, as to save you from greater taxation to save the Union exclusively by other means—

You dislike the emancipation proclamation; and, perhaps, would have it retracted— You say it is unconstitutional— I think differently. I think the Constitution invests its Commander-in-chief, with the law of war in time of war— The most that can be said, if so much, is that slaves are property. Is there— has there ever been— any question that by the law of war, property, both of enemies and friends, may be taken when needed? And is it not needed whenever taking it, helps us, or hurts the enemy? Armies, the world over, destroy enemies property when they can not use it; and even destroy their own to keep it from the enemy— Civilized belligerents do all in their power to keep themselves, or hurt the enemy, except a few things regarded as barbarous or cruel— Among the exceptions are the

Executive Mansion,

Washington   186 .

nor proposed any measure, which is not consistent with

even your view, provided you are for the Union. I suggest-

ed compensated emancipation; to which you replied you

wished not to be taxed to buy negroes. But I had

not asked you to be taxed to buy negroes, except

in such way, as to save you from greater taxation to save

the Union exclusively by other means.

You dislike the emancipation proclamation; and, perhaps,

would have it retracted. You say it is unconstitu-

tional. I think differently. I think the constitution in-

vests it's commander-in-chief, with the law of war in

time of war. The most that can be said, if so much,

is that slaves are property. Is there — has there ever

been — any question that by the law of war, property,

both of enemies and friends, may be taken when need-

ed? And is it not needed whenever taking it, helps

us, or hurts the enemy? Armies, the world over, destroy

enemie's property when they can not use it; and even des-

troy their own to keep it from the enemy. Civilized

beligerents do all in their power to help themselves,

or hurt the enemy, except a few things regarded

as barbarous or cruel. Among the exceptions are the

Looking exhausted but defiant, Lincoln poses for Treasury
Department photographer Lewis E. Walker in Washington
in 1863.

5.

massacre of vanquished foes, and now- combatants, male
and female.

But the proclamation, as law, either is valid, or is not
valid. If it is not valid, it needs no retraction. If it
is valid, it can not be retracted, any more than ~~you can bring~~
can be brought
the dead, to life. Some of you profess to think
it; retraction would operate favorably for the Union- Why
better after the retraction, than before the issue? There
was more than a year and a half of trial to suppress the rebellion before the proclamation issued, the
last one hundred days of which passed under an
explicit notice that it was coming, unless averted by
those in revolt, returning to their allegiance, The war
                                                                    the
has certainly progressed as favorably for us, since ~~the~~ issue
of the proclamation
as before.

'You' say you will not fight to free negroes. Some of them
seem willing to fight for you; but, no matter. Fight you,
then, exclusively to save the Union. I issued the proclamation on purpose to aid you in saving the Union.
Whenever you shall have conquered all resistance
to the Union, if I shall urge you to continue fighting,
                                        then
it will be an apt time, for you to declare you will
not fight to free negroes.

massacres of vanquished foes, and non-combattants, male and female.

But the proclamation, as law, either is valid, or is not valid. If it is not valid, it needs no retraction. If it is valid, it can not be retracted, any more than ~~you~~
can be brought
~~can bring~~ the dead ∧ to life. Some of you profess to think it's retraction would operate favorably for the Union. Why better <u>after</u> the retraction, than <u>before</u> the issue? There was more than a year and a half of trial to suppress the rebellion before the proclamation issued, the last one hundred days of which passed under an explicit notice that it was coming, unless averted by those in revolt, returning to their allegiance. The war
the
has certainly progressed as favorably for us, since ~~it's~~ issue
of the proclamation
as before.

You say you will not fight to free negroes. Some of them seem willing to fight for you; but, no matter. Fight you, then, exclusively to save the Union. I issued the proclamation on purpose to aid you in saving the Union. Whenever you shall have conquered all resistence to the Union, if I shall urge you to continue fighting,
then
it will be an apt time ∧ for you to declare you will not fight to free negroes.

Freshly uniformed African-American soldiers pose for tintype photographs intended for loved ones at home. "The Star Spangled Banner is now the harbinger of Liberty," Frederick Douglass accurately predicted after Lincoln issued his preliminary Emancipation Proclamation, "and the millions in bondage, inured to hardships, accustomed to toil, ready to suffer, ready to fight, to dare and to die, will rally under that banner wherever they see it gloriously unfolded to the breeze." By war's end, some 200,000 black men had served in the Union Army and Navy, fighting in 449 battles and suffering casualties 35 percent greater than white troops.

6.

I thought that ~~that~~ in your struggle for the Union, to whatever extent the negroes should cease helping the enemy, to that extent it weakened the enemy in his resistence to you. Do you think different? I thought that whatever negroes can be got to do as soldiers leaves just so much less for white soldiers to do, in saving the Union. Does it appear otherwise to you? But negroes, like other people, act upon motives. Why should they do any thing for us, if we will do nothing for them? If they stake their lives for us, they must be prompted by the strongest motive—even the promise of freedom. And the promise being made, must be kept.

I thought that ~~that~~ in your struggle for the Union, to

whatever extent the negroes should cease helping the

enemy, to that extent it weakened the enemy in

his resistence to you. Do you think differently? I thought

that whatever negroes can be got to do as soldiers

leaves just so much less for white soldiers to do,

in saving the Union. Does it appear otherwise to you?

But negroes, like other people, act upon motives.

Why should they do any thing for us, if we will

do nothing for them? If they stake their lives for

us, they must be prompted by the strongest motive —

even the promise of freedom. And the promise

being made, must be kept.

STORMING FORT WAGNER.

All but illustrating Lincoln's blunt reminder that "some of them seem willing to fight for you"— meaning so-called "colored troops"—Kurz & Allison's famous chromo shows black soldiers from the legendary 54th Massachusetts, led by white Colonel Robert Gould Shaw, meeting a heroic death at Fort Wagner in 1863.

153

7.

The signs look better. The Father of Waters again goes unvexed to the sea. Thanks to the great North-West for it. Nor yet wholly to them. Three hundred miles up, they met New-England, Empire, Key-Stone, and Jersey, hewing their way right and left. The Sunny South too, in more colors than one, also lent a hand. On the spot their part of the history was jotted down in black and white. The job was a great national one; and let none be banned who bore an honorable part in it. And while those who have cleared the great river may well be proud, even that is not all. It is hard to say that anything has been more bravely, and well done, than at Antietam, Murfreesboro, Gettysburg, and on many fields of lesser note. Nor must Uncle Sam's Web-feet be forgotten. At all the watery margins they have been present. Not only on the deep sea, the broad bay, and the rapid river; but also up the narrow muddy bayou, and wherever the ground was a little damp, they have been, and made their tracks. Thanks to all. For the great republic— for the principle it lives by, and keeps alive— for man's vast future— thanks to all.

The signs look better. The Father of Waters again goes

unvexed to the sea. Thanks to the great North-West

for it. Nor yet wholly to them. Three hundred

miles up, they met New-England, Empire, Key-Stone,
  Jersey,
and ~~the Jerseys~~,' hewing their way right and left.

The Sunny South too, in more colors than one, also

lent a hand. On the spot their part of the histo-

ry was jotted down in black and white. The job

was a great national one; and let none be banned

who bore an honorable part in it. And while

those who have cleared the great river may well
                          It is hard to say that anything
be proud, even that is not all. ~~Nothing~~ has been

more bravely, and well done, than at Antietam,

Murfreesboro, Gettysburg, and on many fields of

lesser note. Nor must Uncle Sam's Web-feet be

forgotten. At all the watery margins they have been

present. Not only on the deep sea, the broad bay,

and the rapid river; but also up the narrow

muddy bayou, and wherever the ground was a lit-

tle damp, they have been, and made their tracks.

Thanks to all. For the great republic — for the

principle it lives by, and keeps alive — for man's

vast future — thanks to all.

A map published around the time of the Lincoln centennial pin-
points the military campaigns of the Civil War. Lincoln, who loved
maps and kept several in his White House office, visited few of the
Southern states shown here, but believed passionately that the
federal union was indivisible. "As to any dread of my having
'a purpose to enslave or exterminate the whites of the South,'"
Lincoln wrote, "I can scarcely believe that such dread exists. It is
absurd."

8.

Peace does not appear so distant as it did. I hope it will come soon, and come to stay; and so come as to be worth the keeping in all future time. It will then have been proven that, among free men, there can be no successful appeal from the ballot to the bullet; and that they who take such appeal are sure to lose their case, and pay the cost. And then, there will be some black men who can remember that, with silent tongue, and clenched teeth, and steady eye, and well poised bayonet, they have helped mankind on to this great consummation; while, I fear, there will be some white ones, unable to forget that, with malignant heart, and deceitful speech, they have strove to hinder it.

Still, let us not be over-sanguine of a speedy final triumph. Let us be quite sober. Let us diligently apply the means, never doubting that a just God, in his own good time, will give us the rightful result.

Yours very truly
A. Lincoln

Peace does not appear so distant as it did. I hope it will come soon, and come to stay; and so come as to be worth the keeping in all future time. It will then have been proved that, among free men, there can be no successful appeal from the ballot to the bullet; and that they who take such appeal are sure to lose their case, and pay the cost. And then, there will be some black men who can remember that, with silent tongue, and clenched teeth, and steady ∧eye, and well ~~borne~~ poised bayonet, they have helped mankind on to this great con-summation; while ∧I fear, there will be some white ones, unable to forget that, with malignant hearts, and deceitful speech, they have strove to hinder it.

Still, let us not be over-sanguine of a speedy final triumph. Let us be quite sober. Let us diligently apply the means, never doubting that a just God, in his own good time, will give us the rightful result.

Yours very truly

A Lincoln

THE BATTLE OF SHARPSBURG, MD SEPT 16TH 1862.

COM. FARRAGUT'S FLEET, PASSING THE FORTS ON THE MISSISSIPPI, APRIL 24TH 1862.
The U.S. Frigate Mississippi destroying the rebel Ram Manassas.

"The signs look better," Lincoln declared in his Springfield message, pointing to Union victories celebrated in period graphics: The Battle of Antietam (or Sharpsburg; a print by Currier & Ives), the Battle of Gettysburg (a sketch by Edwin Forbes), and the capture of the "father of waters," the Mississippi River, as vivified in this Currier & Ives print of Farragut's fleet breaking past Forts Jackson and St. Philip en route to New Orleans.

LETTER TO **CPT. JAMES M. CUTTS, JR.**, OCTOBER 26, 1863

Ever loyal, and characteristically forgiving, the president clearly labored over this rarely cited gem of
literature: advice to the brother-in-law of his late, longtime political enemy, Stephen A. Douglas, as the
young man faced disheartening military discipline.

/

Executive Mansion,

Washington, Oct 26, , 1863 .

Capt. James M. Cutts.

Although what I am now to say to you
is to be, in form, a reprimand, it is not intended to add
a pang to what you have already suffered upon the subject to which it relates— You have too much of life yet
before you, and have shown too much of promise as an
officer, for your future to be lightly surrendered—
You were convicted of two offences— One of them,
not of great enormity, and yet greed, to be avoided, I feel sure you are in no danger of repeat-
ing— The other you are not so ~~sure~~ against— This advice of a father to his son "Beware of entrance
to a quarrel, but being in, ~~a~~ bear it that the
opposed
~~officer~~ may beware of thee" is good, and yet
not the best. Quarrel not at all— No man resolved
to make the most of himself, can spare time
for personal contention— Still less can he afford
to take all the consequences, including the vitiating
of his temper, and the loss of self-control—

Executive Mansion,

Washington, Oct 26, 1863.

Capt. James M. Cutts.

Although what I am now to say ~~to you~~

is to be, in form, a reprimand, it is not intended to add

a pang to what you have already suffered upon the sub-

ject to which it relates. You have too much of life yet

before you, and have shown too much of promise as an

officer, for your future to be lightly surrendered.

You were convicted of two offences. One of them,

not of great enormity, and yet greatly to be avoid-

ed, I feel sure you are in no danger of repeat-

                                        well armed
ing. The other you are not so ~~sure~~ against. The ad-

vice of a father to his son "Beware of entrance

to a quarrel, but being in, ~~so~~ bear it that the
opposed
~~opposer~~ may beware of thee" is good, and yet

not the best. Quarrel not at all. No man resolved

to make the most of himself, can spare time

for personal contention. Still less can he afford

to take all the consequences, including the vitiating

of his temper, and the loss of self-control.

$\mathcal{D}$ORIS KEARNS GOODWIN

The young army officer to whom Lincoln addressed this gentle note had been court-martialed for "conduct unbecoming an officer and a gentleman," and sentenced to dismissal from the service. Taking into account the "previous good character" of Captain Cutts, Lincoln had reduced the sentence to a reprimand. The first charge against Cutts—that he had been found peeping through a blind at a lady undressing in a neighboring room—Lincoln considered "not of great enormity." Indeed, he later jokingly suggested that Cutts "should be elevated to the peerage for it with the title of Count Peeper." The second charge—that his intemperate words in addressing a superior officer had almost led to a duel—was more serious, demanding the reprimand.

Yet, in the very first sentence, Lincoln reveals what may have been the most important of his emotional strengths—his unusual empathy, his gift of putting himself in the place of others, for he tells Cutts that the reprimand "is not intended to add a pang to what you have already suffered," but instead is to be seen as the advice of a wise father to a son: "No man resolved to make the most of himself," Lincoln writes, "can spare time for personal contention." The advice comes from the heart. All his life, Lincoln tried to avoid petty grievances. He refused to submit to jealousy or to brood over perceived slights.

(continued)

Yield larger things, to which you can show no more than equal right; and yield lesser ones, though clearly your own. Better give your path to a dog, than be bitten by him in contesting for the right. Even killing the dog would not cure the bite.

In the mood indicated deal henceforth with your fellow men, and especially with your brother officers, and even the unpleasant events you are passing from will not have been profitless to you.

Yield larger things to which you can show no more than equal right; and yield lesser ones, though clearly your own. Better give your path to a dog, than be bitten by him in contesting for the right. Even killing the dog would not cure the bite.

In the mood indicated deal henceforth with your fellow man, and especially with your brother officers; and even the unpleasant events you are passing from will not have been profitless to you.

"Better give your path to a dog, than be bitten by him contesting for the right. Even killing the dog would not cure the bite." Here Lincoln's literary and storytelling skills are on full display. With concrete, visual language, he forcefully and memorably illustrates his point.

Then, in closing, he affectionately suggests that if the young officer can learn from his painful experience, "the unpleasant events . . . will not have been profitless." Cutts returned to the army, and served with great distinction. ◄

Though Cutts—a white man—went virtually unpunished for his offenses
as a Peeping Tom, black soldiers convicted of sexual offenses against white women were dealt with harshly,
as this horrifying execution scene attests. It was likely taken, and circulated,
to discourage other potential offenders.

GETTYSBURG ADDRESS, NOVEMBER 19, 1863

What Lincoln said at Gettysburg is fixed like stone in American memory. But Lincoln's words were far from fixed. Even after he delivered the speech, he continued to revise it, showing close attention to rhythm and nuance. This, the so-called Hay Copy, is probably the second draft. Historians remain unsure about which copy Lincoln actually read from, but the many drafts make it clear the president did not write the speech in haste on the train, as legend stubbornly insists.

Four score and seven years ago our fathers brought forth, upon this continent, a new nation, conceived in Liberty, and dedicated to the proposition that all men are created equal.

Now we are engaged in a great civil war, testing whether that nation, or any nation, so conceived, and so dedicated, can long endure. We are met here on a great battle-field of that war. We have come to dedicate a portion of it as a final resting place for those who here gave their lives that that nation might live. It is altogether fitting and proper that we should do this.

But in a larger sense we can not dedicate — we can not consecrate — we can not hallow this ground. The brave men, living and dead, who struggled here, have consecrated it far above our poor power to add or detract. The world will little note, nor long remember, what we say here, but can never forget what they did here. It is for us, the living, rather to be dedicated here to the unfinished work which they have, thus far, so nobly carried on. It is rather

Four score and seven years ago our fathers

brought forth, upon this continent, a new nation, con-

ceived in Liberty, and dedicated to the proposition

that all men are created equal.

Now we are engaged in a great civil war, test-

ing whether that nation, or any nation, so conceived,

and so dedicated, can long endure. We are met

here on a great battle-field of that war. We ~~are~~ have
come
~~met~~ to dedicate a portion of it as ~~the~~ a final rest-
for
ing place ~~of~~ those who here gave their lives that

that nation might live. It is altogether fitting

and proper that we should do this.

But in a larger sense we can not dedicate —

we can not consecrate — we can not hallow this

ground. The brave men, living and dead, who strug-
poor
gled here, have consecrated it far above our ∧ power

to add or detract. The world will little note,

nor long remember, what we say here, but

can never forget what they did here. It is

for us, the living, rather to be dedicated
work
here to the unfinished ∧ which they have,

thus far, so nobly carried on. It is rather

ᴛ ONI MORRISON

When a president of the United States thought about the graveyard his country had become, and said, "The world will little note, nor long remember, what we say here, but can never forget what they did here," his simple words were exhilarating in their life-sustaining properties because they refused to encapsulate the reality of 600,000 dead men in a cataclysmic race war.

Refusing to monumentalize, disdaining the "final word," the precise "summing up," acknowledging their "poor power to add or detract," his words signal deference to the uncapturability of the life they mourn. It is the deference that moves here, that recognition that language can never live up to life once and for all. Nor should it. Language can never "pin down" slavery, genocide, war. Nor should it yearn for the arrogance to be able to do so. Its force, its felicity, is in its reach toward the ineffable. ◄

A newly unearthed photograph shows a top-hatted man on horseback—likely Lincoln himself—nearing the speaker's platform at Gettysburg on November 19, 1863.

for us to be here dedicated to the great
task remaining before us— that from these
honored dead we take increased devotion
to the cause for which they here gave
the last full measure of devotion— that
we here highly resolve that these dead
shall not have died in vain; that this
nation shall have a new birth of freedom;
and that this government of the people, by
the people, for the people, shall not perish
from the earth.

for us to be here dedicated to the great

task remaining before ^{us}_∧— that from these

honored dead we take increased devotion

    that
to ~~the~~ cause for which they here gave ~~gave~~

the last full measure of devotion — that

we here highly resolve that these dead

shall not have died in vain; that this

nation shall have a new birth of freedom;

and that this government of the people, by

the people, for the people, shall not perish

from the earth.

Lincoln poses for photographer Alexander Gardner
eleven days before delivering the Gettysburg Address.

Bareheaded, President Lincoln
takes his place on the speaker's
platform at the new Gettysburg
National Cemetery on November
19, 1863. Hours will pass—filled
with hymns and orations—before
he finally rises to deliver his two
minutes of "appropriate remarks."

On March 4, 1864, Michael Hahn was elected governor of Louisiana, which became the first of the seceded states to organize a government committed to the Union. Eleven days later, Lincoln wrote Hahn to make known, gingerly, his instincts on black suffrage.

Private   Executive Mansion,

Washington, March 13. , 1864.

Hon. Michael Hahn

    My dear Sir:

        I congratulate you on having fixed your name in history as the first free-state Governor of Louisiana. Now you are about to have a Convention, which among other things, will probably define the elective franchise— I barely suggest for your private consideration, whether some of the colored people may not be let in— as, for instance, the very intelligent, and especially those who have fought gallantly in our ranks. They would probably help, in some trying time to come, to keep the jewel of liberty within the family of freedom. But this is only a suggestion, not to the public, but to you alone.

          Yours truly

          A. Lincoln

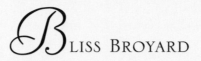

BLISS BROYARD

Executive Mansion,

Washington, March 13., 1864.

Hon. Michael Hahn

My dear Sir:

I congratulate you on having fixed

your name in history as the first free-state Governor of

Louisiana. Now you are about to have a Conven-

tion, which among other things, will probably define

the elective franchise. I barely suggest for your private

consideration, whether some of the colored people may

not be let in — as, for instances, the very intelligent,

and especially those who have fought gallantly in

our ranks. They would probably help, in some trying

time to come, to keep the jewell of liberty within

the family of freedom. But this is only a sugges-

tion, not to the public, but to you alone.

Yours truly

A. Lincoln

In 2001, at a conference on the Louisiana Native Guard, a Civil War regiment of black and colored men, I met Julie Hilla, an older white woman with short wavy hair, round librarian glasses, and merry eyes. I figured her for a genealogist or researcher. But when I told her that my great-great-grandfather had fought with the colored troops, she surprised me. "So you're mixed too!" she exclaimed.

Julie, like me, had grown up unaware of her African ancestry. When we met, I had known about my dad's Creole background for eleven years. Julie had only just found out, at seventy-eight. She had long known her grandfather was an early civil rights activist and was tickled to read, in a book on New Orleans history, how Arnold Bertonneau visited President Lincoln to petition for black suffrage. But when she saw her grandfather described as "a colored gentleman," she told her husband that the author must be mistaken. She found out later that she'd long been deceived.

The day after meeting with Julie's grandfather and his associate, Lincoln wrote this letter to Louisiana's governor; the governor ignored his suggestion that "some of the colored people" be let into the franchise. When Lincoln repeated his desire for black suffrage in a speech marking the end of the war, John Wilkes Booth declared he'd kill him.

Back in Louisiana, following a short-lived Reconstruction, Bertonneau challenged the segregation of his children's elementary school. After losing the suit, he left New Orleans for California, where Julie's mother would be raised as white. But unlike many families who never look back after crossing the color line, the Bertonneaus kept alive the memory of their grandfather—and his brush with history. ◄

In this careful letter, Lincoln narrated the history of his ideas and actions on American slavery.
The letter combines a declaration of personal sentiments, a constitutional argument,
and, in the end, a nervy theological claim.

Executive Mansion,

Washington, April 4 , 1864.

A. G. Hodges, Esq
Frankfort, Ky.
My dear Sir:

You ask me to put in writing the substance
of what I verbally said the other day, in your presence, to Governor Bramlette and Senator Dixon— It was about as follows;
"I am naturally anti-slavery. If slavery is not wrong, nothing
is wrong. I can not remember when I did not so think, and
feel. And yet I have never understood that the Presidency
conferred upon me an unrestricted right to act officially
upon this judgment and feeling. It was in the oath
I took that I would, to the best of my ability, preserve,
protect, and defend the Constitution of the United States.
I could not take the office without taking the oath.
Nor was it my view that I might take an oath to get
power, and break the oath in using the power, I understood, too, that in ordinary civil administration this oath
even forbade me to practically indulge my primary abstract
judgment on the moral question of slavery. I had publicly declared this many times, and in many ways. And I aver
that, to this day, I have done no official act in mere
deference to my abstract judgment and feeling on slavery.
I did understand however, that my oath to preserve the Constitution to the best of my ability, imposed upon me the duty of
preserving, by every indispensable means, that government— that
nation— of which that Constitution was the organic law. Was
it possible to lose the nation, and yet preserve the Constitution?

Executive Mansion,

Washington, April 4, 1864.

A. G. Hodges, Esq

Frankfort, Ky.

My dear Sir:

You ask me to put in writing the substance of what I verbally said the other day, in yours presence, to Governor Bramlette and Senator Dixon. It was about as follows:

"I am naturally anti-slavery. If slavery is not wrong, nothing is wrong. I can not remember when I did not so think, and feel. And yet I have never understood that the Presidency conferred upon me an unrestricted right to act officially upon this judgment and feeling. It was in the oath I took that I would, to the best of my ability, preserve, protect, and defend the Constitution of the United States. I could not take the office without taking the oath. Nor was it my view that I might take an oath to get power, and break the oath using the power. I understood, too, that in ordinary civil administration this oath even forbade me to practically indulge my primary abstract judgment on the moral question of slavery. I had publicly declared this many times, and in many ways. And I aver that, to this day, I have done no official act in mere deference to my abstract judgment and feeling on slavery.

however,

I did understand ~~hower~~, that my oath to preserve the Cons-
to
titution ∧ the best of my ability, imposed upon me the duty of preserving, by every indispensable means, that government — that nation — of which that Constitution was the organic law. Was
yet
it possible to lose the nation, and ∧ preserve the Constitution?

Lincoln magnifies as he comes down the ages. The momentum of his collected words reminds us of those better angels he tried to summon, the difference between his actual achievements and those we too generously and posthumously bestow on him, our own collective wish for ourselves. But Lincoln is first and foremost a wholly political animal, tacking furiously this way and that to find those elusive gusts that would propel him (and us) forward. Nowhere is this more evident than in his famous letter to Albert Hodges, written in early April of 1864. In retrospect we impose on Mr. Lincoln the simplistic virtues of a Hollywood hero, a crusading "Mr. Smith" who goes to Washington to free the slaves and reset America's course, and not the shrewd western politician he actually was. But as this slippery letter to a border-state newspaperman shows, Lincoln was nearly always willing to continue his abstraction of slavery (an abstraction that so disappointed Frederick Douglass and others) to mollify his border-state allies and keep himself firmly within his political mentor Henry Clay's anachronistic worldview.

(continued)

By general law life and limb must be protected; yet often a limb must be amputated to save a life; but a life is never wisely given to save a limb. I felt that measures, otherwise unconstitutional, might become lawful, by becoming indispensable to the preservation of the Constitution, through the preservation of the nation. Right or wrong, I assumed this ground, and now avow it. I could not feel that, to the best of my ability, I had even tried to preserve the Constitution, if, to save slavery, or any minor matter, I should permit the wreck of government, country, and Constitution all together. When, early in the war, Gen. Fremont attempted military emancipation, I forbade it, because I did not then think it an indispensable necessity. When a little later, Gen. Cameron, then Secretary of War, suggested the arming of the blacks, I objected, because I did not yet think it an indispensable necessity. When, still later, Gen. Hunter attempted military emancipation, I again forbade it, because I did not yet think the indispensable necessity had come. When, in March, and May, and July 1862 I made earnest, and successive appeals to the border states to favor compensated emancipation, I believed the indispensable necessity for military emancipation, and arming the blacks would come, unless averted by that measure. They declined the proposition; and I was, in my best judgment, driven to the alternative of either surrendering the Union, and with it, the Constitution, or of laying strong hand upon the colored element. I chose the latter. In choosing it, I hoped for greater gain than loss; but of this, I was

By general law life <u>and</u> limb must be protected; yet often a limb must be amputated to save a life; but a life is never wisely given to save a limb. I felt that measures, otherwise unconstitutional, might become lawful, by becoming indispensable to the preservation of the Constitution, through the preservation of the nation. Right or wrong, I assumed this ground, and now avow it. I could not feel that, to the best of my ability, I had even tried to preserve the Constitution, if, to save slavery, or any minor matter, I should permit the wreck of government, country, and ~~Constution~~ Constitution all together. When, early in the war, Gen. Fremont attempted military emancipation, I forbade it, because I did not then think it an indispensable necessity. When a little later, Gen. Cameron, then Secretary of War, suggested the arming of the blacks, I objected, because I did not yet think it an indispensable necessity. When, still later, Gen. Hunter attempted military emancipation, I again forbade it, because I did not yet think the indispensable necessity had come. When, in March, and May, and July 1862 I made earnest, and successive appeals to the border states to favor compensated emancipation, I believed the indispensable necessity for military emancipation, and arming the blacks would come, unless averted by that measure, They declined the proposition; and I was, in my best judgment, driven to the alternative of either surrendering the Union, and with it, the Constitution, or of laying strong hand upon the colored element. I chose the latter. In choosing it, I hoped for greater gain than loss; but of this, I was

The famous phrase from this letter ". . . yet often a limb must be amputated to save a life; but a life is never wisely given to save a limb . . ." is often cited as expressing the excruciating calculus that placed the survival of the Union, and not the immediate emancipation of the slaves, as paramount in Lincoln's efforts. But what that phrase, and indeed the whole letter, more accurately reflects, is the tension in Lincoln's own view of the law. (That tension informs nearly all of his tortured debates about slavery from the beginning of his career.) Lincoln, once again, carefully parses the difference between "natural" law, and the total and unequivocal repudiation of slavery that natural law suggests, and the man-made or "positive" laws he believes the Constitution requires him to obey above all else. Stubbornly embedded among those "positive" laws are of course the ones that have perpetuated the institution of slavery, an institution Lincoln continually claims to abhor. Despite having invoked the Declaration of Independence's obvious appeal to natural laws in his celebrated address at Gettysburg the previous November, Lincoln here reverts to a more careful argument that will bedevil abolitionists, perhaps mollify those border-state sympathies requiring more gradual emancipation, and do nothing to quell the ardor of the separationists in rebellion. Lost in all the parsing, of course, are the four million Americans owned by other Americans, whose lives, once again, have been reduced to merely a legal interpretation, albeit a well-reasoned and well-intentioned one, by our Great Liberator. ◄

not entirely confident. More than a year of trial now shows no loss by it in our foreign relations, none in our home popular sentiment, none in our white military force,—no loss by it any how, or any where. On the contrary, it shows a gain of quite a hundred and thirty thousand soldiers, seamen, and laborers. These are palpable facts, about which, as facts, there can be no caviling. We have the men; and we could not have had them without the measure.

And now let any Union man who complains of the measure, test himself by writing down in one line that he is for subduing the rebellion by force of arms; and in the next, that he is for taking these hundred and thirty thousand men from the Union side, and placing them where they would be but for the measure he condemns. If he can not face his case so stated, it is only because he can not face the truth.

I add a word which was not in the verbal conversation. In telling this tale I attempt no compliment to my own sagacity. I claim not to have controlled events, but confess plainly that events have controlled me. Now, at the end of three years struggle the nation's condition is not what either party, or any man devised, or expected. God alone can claim it. Whither it is tending seems plain. If God now wills the removal of a great wrong, and wills also that we of the North as well as you of the South, shall pay fairly for our complicity in that wrong, impartial history will find therein new cause to attest and revere the justice and goodness of God.

Yours truly

A. Lincoln

not entirely confident. More than a year of trial now shows

no loss by it in our foreign relations, none in our home popu-

lar sentiment, none in our white military force, — no loss

by it any how, or _∧ ^{any} where. On the contrary, it shows a gain

of quite a hundred and thirty thousand soldiers, seamen,

and laborers. There are palpable facts, about which, as facts,

there can be no cavilling. We have the men; and we

could not have had them without the measure.

And now let any Union man who complains of the meas-

ure, test himself by writing down in one line that he is for

subduing the rebellion by force of arms; and in the next, that

he is for taking these hundred and thirty thousand men from

the Union side, and placing them where they would be but

for the measures he condemns. If he can not face his case

so stated, it is only because he can not face the truth.

I add a word which was not in the verbal conversa-

tion. In telling _∧ ^{this} tale I attempt no compliment to my own

sagacity. I claim not to have controlled events, but confess

plainly that events have controlled me. Now, at the end

of three years struggle the nation's condition is not what either

party, or any man devised, or expected. God alone can claim

it. Whither it is tending seems plain. If God now wills the

removal of a great wrong, and wills also that we of the North

as well as you of the South, shall pay fairly for our complicity

in that wrong, impartial history will find therein ~~no~~ ^{new} cause

to ~~question~~ the justice ~~or~~ ^{and} goodness of God.

attest and revere ^{~~applaud~~}

Yours truly

A. Lincoln

Rev. Phineas Densmore Gurley held the pulpit at
Washington's New York Avenue Presbyterian Church,
where Lincoln often worshipped. "I like Gurley," the
president explained. "He don't preach politics. I get
enough of that through the week, and when I go to church,
I like to hear the gospel."

Long an outspoken critic, Frederick Douglass visited
Lincoln in the White House to demand that black
enlistees receive equal pay. "I assure you, Mr. Douglass,"
Lincoln replied, "that in the end they shall have the same
pay as white soldiers...." The abolitionist later admitted
that, compared to his racist fellow countrymen, Lincoln
was "swift, zealous, radical, and determined."

ABRAHAM LINCOLN'S

ECEPTION.

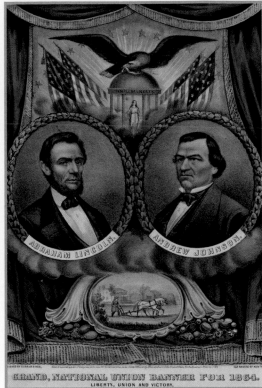

GRAND, NATIONAL UNION BANNER FOR 1864.
LIBERTY, UNION AND VICTORY.

Lincoln's quest for a second term inspired fewer prints than the first—but that was because by 1864 he was so well known. This Currier & Ives banner suggested through its symbolic design that a Lincoln victory would usher in an era of economic prosperity.

The "grand White House reception" depicted in this oversize display print honored the newly promoted Lieutenant General Ulysses S. Grant in 1864. Even in the darkest days of the war, Lincoln and his wife (except for the time she secluded herself in mourning for her late son Willie) maintained a surprisingly vigorous social schedule of public levees, diplomatic receptions, dinners, outdoor concerts, and other events.

In Ulysses S. Grant, Lincoln finally found a general as tenacious as he, and together they enacted a ruthless strategy to destroy the Confederate armies and collapse Southern morale. These brief dispatches show Lincoln in sync with his general—though not without humor.

"Copy"

Executive Mansion,

Washington, August 17, 1864.

Lieut. Gen. Grant
        City Point, Va.

    I have seen your despatch expressing your unwillingness to break your hold where you are. Neither am I willing. Hold on with a bull-dog grip, and chew & choke, as much as possible.

                                A. Lincoln

Head Quarters Armies of the United States,
                City-Point, April 7. 11. Am 1865.

Lieut. Gen. Grant.

    Gen. Sheridan says "If the thing is pressed I think that Lee will surrender." Let the thing be pressed.

                            A. Lincoln

The original dispatch sent by Mr. Lincoln to me, Apl. 7th 1865.
                        U. S. Grant

"Cypher"

Executive Mansion,

Washington, August 17., 1864.

Lieut. Gen. Grant

City Point, Va.

I have seen your despatch express

ing your unwillingness to break your hold where you are.

Neither am I willing. Hold on with a bull-dog

gripe, and chew & choke, as much as possible.

A. Lincoln

Head Quarters Armies of the United States,

City-Point, April 7, 11. Am. 1865

Lieut Gen. Grant.

Gen. Sheridan says "If the thing

is pressed I think that Lee will surrender." Let

the thing be pressed.

A. Lincoln

The original dispatch sent by

Mr. Lincoln to me Apl 7th 1865,

U. S. Grant

ℭONAN O'BRIEN

Lincoln was a great hero, obviously, for myriad reasons—he was a political genius and forward-thinking philosopher. But you could also make a case that he was up there with Twain as a great comic writer of his time.

The second of these two telegrams to Grant is one of my favorite examples. At the end of the Civil War, when Lee was being routed, Sheridan sent a telegram to Lincoln that said, "If the thing is pressed" —meaning, if Grant pursues him—"I think that Lee will surrender." Lincoln replied with a telegram that said, "Let the thing be pressed."

It's so simple. It's brilliant. It's like a *Seinfeld* bit. I can almost hear George Costanza say, "Actually, we could actually get a million dollars if the thing was pressed." And Jerry saying, "Uh, let the thing be pressed." Lincoln had the key qualities of a comedian—his language was tight and surprising. And he was doing this in the 1860s, at a time when people tended to take forever to get to the point and took themselves very seriously. Not only that, but he wrote his own material. Who does that anymore? Whenever you hear a president say something funny, a day later they're always interviewing the guy who actually wrote it. ◄

On August 22, one of Lincoln's closest advisors told him he would lose reelection in November, in part because of a public perception that he could end the war were it not for his abolitionism. On August 23, Lincoln asked members of his cabinet to sign this declaration— but he folded the paper so that they couldn't read it.

Executive Mansion
Washington, Aug 23, 1864.

This morning, as for some days past, it seems exceedingly probable that this Administration will not be re-elected. Then it will be my duty to so co-operate with the President elect, as to save the Union between the election and the inauguration; as he will have secured his election on such ground that he cannot possibly save it afterwards.

A. Lincoln

William H Seward
W. P. Fessenden
Edwin M Stanton
Gideon Welles
Edw. Bates
M Blair
J. P. Usher

August 23. 1864.

Executive Mansion

Washington, Aug 23, 1864.

This morning, as for some days past,

it seems exceedingly probable that

this Administration will not be re-

elected. Then it will be my duty

to so co-operate with the President

elect, as to save the Union between

the election and the inauguration;

as he will have secured his elect-

ion on such ground that he can not

possibly save it afterwards.

A. Lincoln

[Endorsed on Reverse:]
William H Seward
W. P. Fessenden
Edwin M Stanton
Gideon Welles
Edwd. Bates

M Blair

J. P. Usher

August 23 1864.

*P*HILIP GOUREVITCH

Most of the civil wars that tear at our world today are, above all, wars of succession. What is at issue is the transfer of power from one leader and his followers to the next party. The ones with power won't let go, and the ones without won't give up. So they fight, and the country that both sides claim to rule is destroyed in the clash. The evocation of "military necessity" becomes the justification for the leader of each side to hold on to power more relentlessly than ever.

How extraordinary, then, to imagine President Lincoln in the desolate summer of 1864, as he fought a civil war and a reelection campaign simultaneously. By August of that year, every indication—military and political—was that Lincoln would lose on both fronts. The temptation to suspend elections must have been powerful. But the electoral process and the Union were inseparable, and Lincoln recognized that to win his fight to preserve the Union he might have to lose his office. That is the drama behind the "Blind Memo." The destiny of the Union was greater than the president's personal destiny, and no political passion could be allowed to interfere if the will of the people turned against him.

Lincoln saw what was at stake, but he was not sure that his cabinet members could stand to see it, which is why he folded the memo up and made them sign it without knowing what it said. That is what it means to lead, and what it means to serve. The crease marks—like those that carved ever more deeply into Lincoln's face with each year of his presidency—tell the story. ◄

On September 4, Lincoln anticipated the mood and the theme of his Second Inaugural Address in a letter
to the distinguished Quaker Eliza P. Gurney. The two had visited together and shared prayers
"for wisdom on high" in 1862. Lincoln confided that day that he believed America was going through what
he called "a fiery trial" willed by God.

Executive Mansion,

Washington, September 4, 1864.

Eliza P. Gurney.
My esteemed friend.

I have not forgotten—
probably never shall forget— the very
impressive occasion when yourself
and friends visited me on a Sabbath
forenoon two years ago, Nor has your
kind letter, written nearly a year later,
ever been forgotten, In all, it has been
your purpose to strengthen my reliance
on God. I am much indebted to the
good Christian people of the country for
their constant prayers and consolations;
and to no one of them more than to
yourself— The purposes of the Almighty are perfect, and must prevail, though we
erring mortals may fail to accurately perceive them in advance, We hoped for
a happy termination of this terrible war
long before this; but God knows best, and has
ruled otherwise. We shall yet acknowledge
his His wisdom, and our own error therein— Meanwhile we must work earnestly
in the best lights He gives us, trusting that

Executive Mansion,

Washington, September 4, 1864.

Eliza P. Gurney

esteemed
My ~~dear~~ friend.

I have not forgotten —
probably never shall forget — the very
                            when
impressive occasion ~~of the visit of~~ your-
                            visited
self and friends ∧~~to~~ me on a Sabbath

forenoon two years ago. Nor has your

kind letter, written nearly a year later,

ever been forgotten. In all, it has been

your purpose to strengthen my reliance

on God. I am much indebted to the

good christian people of the country for

their constant prayers and consolations;

and to no one of them more than to-
                            the Almighty
yourself. The purposes of ~~God~~ are per-

fect, and must prevail, though we

erring mortals may fail to accurately per-

ceive them in advance. We hoped for

a happy termination of this terrible war
long before
~~ere~~ this; but God knows best, and has
                            acknowledge
ruled otherwise. We shall yet ~~perceive~~

~~his~~ His wisdom, and our own error there-

in. Meanwhile we must work earnestly
  in   us,   that
~~by~~ ∧the best lights He gives, ∧trusting ∧so

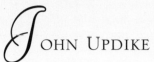

JOHN UPDIKE

The handwriting is unmannered and clear—free, down to its signature, of ostentatious flourishes and signs of the haste for which the president of a nation at war with itself might have been forgiven. Though his penmanship picks up speed on the second page, and a few words, such as "some have chosen one horn and some the other" require a moment's deciphering (right after the missive's one misspelling, "dilema"), the overall impression is one of patience and delicacy, as the writer adjusts his personal tact and warmth to the grave considerations involved in addressing a pious Quaker lady. He stiffens the rote intimacy of "dear" to a more politicized "esteemed"; he distances "God" into "the Almighty"; and, as the commander in chief of cruelly bloodied armies, he reminds Mrs. Gurney that oppression (and no sect was more abolitionist than the pacifist Quakers) can only be "practically" opposed by war.

(continued)

Quaker leader
Eliza P. Gurney praised Lincoln
for his Emancipation
Proclamation, quoting scripture
to declare that it "burst the bands
of wickedness, and let the
oppressed go free."

181

working still conduces to the great
ends he ordains. Surely He intends some
great good to follow this mighty con=
vulsion, which no mortal could
make, and no mortal could stay=
ded.

Your people— the Friends— have
had, and are having, a very great
trial. On principles and faith opposed to both
war and oppression, they can
only practically oppose oppression by war.
In this hard dilema some have chosen
one horn and some the other. For
those appealing to me on conscientious
grounds, I have done, and shall do,
the best I could and can, in my own conscience,
under my oath to the law. That
you believe this I doubt not; and believe=
ing it, I shall still receive, for our
country and myself, your earnest prayers
to our common Father in Heaven.

Your sincere friend.

A. Lincoln

working still conduces to the great

ends He ordains. Surely He intends some

great good to follow this mighty con-

vulsion, which no mortal could

make, and no mortal could ~~hin~~ stay

~~der~~.

Your people — the Friends — have

had, and are having, a very great

trial. On principle, opposed to both and faith

war <u>and</u> oppression, they can

only ∧ oppose oppression by war. practically

In this hard dilema some have chosen

one horn and some the other. For

those appealing to me on conscientious

grounds, I have done, and shall do,

the best I ∧ can, in my own conscience, could and

under my oath to the law. That

you ~~know~~ this I doubt not; and ~~know~~- believe believ-

ing it, I shall still receive, for our

country and myself, your earnest prayers

to our ~~common~~ Father in Heaven,

Your sincere friend,

A. Lincoln

He trusts her to "believe," since she cannot "know," that his own conscience is engaged, under his oath to the law, with the immense question, later posed in his second inaugural address, of God's purposes in "this terrible war." To know that a war is terrible and yet steadfastly to prosecute it is a leader's burden. He accepts her Christian prayers yet holds to his course in "this mighty convulsion, which no mortal could make, and no mortal could stay"—the monosyllabic verb more biblically stark than "hinder" and reverberent with the tragic sense that breathes through Lincoln's wartime correspondence. ◀

Burying the dead, Fredericksburg, Virginia, May 1864.

SECOND INAUGURAL ADDRESS, MARCH 4, 1865

"I expect it to wear," Lincoln wrote of his Second Inaugural, "as well as—perhaps better than—any thing I have produced." Recognizing that many would object to its invocation of divine retribution to explain the sufferings produced by the war, he shrugged: "It is a truth which I thought needed to be told."

Fellow Countrymen.

At this second appearing to take the oath of the presidential office, there is less occasion for an extended address than there was at the first. Then a statement, somewhat in detail, of a course to be pursued, seemed fitting and proper. Now, at the expiration of four years, during which public declarations have been constantly called forth on every point and phase of the great contest which still absorbs the attention, and engrosses the energies of the nation, little that is new could be presented. The progress of our arms, upon which all else chiefly depends, is as well known to the public as to myself; and it is, I trust, reasonably satisfactory and encouraging to all. With high hope for the future, no prediction in regard to it is ventured.

On the occasion corresponding to this four years ago, all thoughts were anxiously directed to an impending civil war. All dreaded it—all sought to avert it. While the inaugeral address was being delivered from this place, devoted altogether to saving the Union without war, insurgent agents were in

Fellow Countrymen

At this second appearing to take the oath of the presidential office, there is less occasion for an extended address than there was at the first. Then a statement, somewhat in detail, of a course to be pursued, seemed fitting and proper. Now, at the expiration of four years, during which public declarations have been constantly called forth on every point and phase of the great contest which still absorbs the attention, and engrosses the enerergies of the nation, little that is new could be presented. The progress of our arms, upon which all else chiefly depends, is as well known to the public as to myself; and it is, I trust, reasonably satisfactory and encouraging to all. With high hope for the future, no prediction in regard to it is ventured.

On the occasion corresponding to this four years ago, all thoughts were anxiously directed to an impending civil war. All dreaded it — all sought to avert it. While the inaugeral address was being delivered from this place, devoted altogether to <u>saving</u> the Union without war, insurgent agents were in

$\mathcal{H}$ENRY LOUIS GATES, JR.

On March 4, 1865, Lincoln delivered what for Frederick Douglass, and many other African Americans, was his most resonant speech, a speech more about them and for them than any of Lincoln's other speeches or writings, even the Emancipation Proclamation: 703 words, as historian Ted Widmer has pointed out, 505 of which were of one syllable, in just twenty-five sentences. It lasted all of six minutes. But in three distinct sections of his third paragraph, Lincoln pronounced, more powerfully than he ever had, the freedom of the Negro as the inextricable cause of the war that would soon grind to an end—a war that had left 623,000 Americans dead.

It is safe to say that never before in the history of the American presidency has the political economy of suffering, the rhetoric of a white eye for a black eye, been applied to the condition of the black enslaved. No wonder the reporter of *The Times of London* was struck by the call-and-response of Lincoln's black audience, the shouts and murmurs of "bless the Lord" and similar phrases still familiar in the black church, which must have reached a crescendo as he hit his stride in that remarkable third paragraph.

Frederick Douglass later would note "a leaden stillness" about the white half of the crowd. For black folks in attendance that day, Abraham Lincoln had come home, and blacks had every reason to believe that, at long

(continued)

the city seeking to destroy it without war seeking to dissolve the Union, and divide effects, by negotiation. Both parties deprecated war; but one
of them would make war rather than let the
nation survive; and the other would accept
war rather than let it perish. And the war
came.

One eighth of the whole
population were colored slaves, not distributed generally over the Union, but localized
in the Southern part of it. These slaves constituted a peculiar and powerful interest.
All knew that this interest was, somehow,
the cause of the war. To strengthen, perpetuate, and extend this interest was the object for which the insurgents would rend
the Union, even by war; while the government claimed no right to do more than
to restrict the territorial enlargement of it.
Neither party expected for the war, the magnitude, or the duration, which it has already
attained. Neither anticipated that

186

the city seeking to <u>destroy</u> it without war — seeking to dissole the Union, and divide effects, by negotiation. Both parties deprecated war; but one of them would <u>make</u> war rather than let the nation survive; and the other would <u>accept</u> war rather than let it perish. And the war came.

        One eighth of the whole population were colored slaves, not distributed generally over the Union, but localized in the Southern ∧ <s>half</s> of it. These slaves constituted a peculiar and powerful interest. All knew that this interest was, somehow, the cause of the war. To strengthen, perpetuate, and extend this interest was the object for which the insurgents would rend the Union, even by war; while the government claimed no right to do more than to restrict the territorial enlargement of it. Neither party expected for the war, the magnitude, or the duration, which it has already attained. Neither anticipated that

last, they had found a permanent home in America as freedmen at last. On that day, within that third paragraph, Lincoln became the President of black men and women, far more so than he had even through the Emancipation. No wonder Douglass, who had to fight his way past two racist guards to gain entrance to the White House immediately following the speech, told the president in response to his questioning: "Mr. Lincoln, that was a sacred effort." ◄

Following his inaugural address, newly confirmed Chief Justice Salmon P. Chase—only recently drummed out of the cabinet after plotting unsuccessfully to deny Lincoln renomination, then named to the bench anyway—administers the oath of office. The scene was sketched by an artist for *Harper's Weekly*.

the cause of the conflict might cease with, or even before, the conflict itself should cease. Each looked for an easier triumph, and a result less fundamental and astounding. Both read the same Bible, and pray to the same God; and each invokes His aid against the other. It may seem strange that any men should dare to ask a just God's assistance in wringing their bread from the sweat of other men's faces; but let us judge not that we be not judged. The prayers of both could not be answered; that of neither has been answered fully. The Almighty has His own purposes. "Woe unto the world because of offences! for it must needs be that offences come; but woe to that man by whom the offence cometh!" If we shall suppose that American Slavery is one of those offences which, in the providence of God, must needs come, but which, having continued through His appointed time, He now wills to remove, and that He gives to both North and South, this terrible war, as the woe due to those

the <u>cause</u> of the conflict might cease with, or
even before, the conflict itself should cease. Each
looked for an easier triumph, and a result less
fundamental and astounding. Both read the same
Bible, and pray to the same God; and each invokes His aid against the other. It may seem
strange that any men should dare to ask a just
God's assistance in wringing their bread from
the sweat of other men's faces; but let us judge
not that we be not judged. The prayers of
both could not be answered; that of neither
has been answered fully. The Almighty has His
own purposes. "Woe unto the world because
of offences! for it must needs be that offences come; but woe to that man by whom
the offence cometh!" If we shall suppose
that American Slavery is one of those offences
which, in the providence of God, must needs
come, but which, having continued through
His appointed time, He now wills to remove,
and that He gives to both North and South,
this terrible war, as the woe due to those

Waiting his turn to speak at his inaugural, Abraham Lincoln sits on the South
Portico of the U.S. Capitol on March 4, 1865. This and the photograph below
were taken on the scene by Alexander Gardner.

As the sun bursts forth from cloudy skies—making "my heart jump," the
president admitted—Lincoln, towering above a little white lectern, reads one of
his greatest speeches to a huge throng assembled on the plaza below.

by whom the offence came, shall we discern therein any departure from those divine attributes
which the believers in a Living God always
ascribe to Him? Fondly do we hope— fervent=
ly do we pray— that this mighty scourge of
war may speedily pass away. Yet, if God
wills that it continue, until all the wealth
piled by the bond-man's two hundred and
fifty years of unrequited toil shall be sunk,
and until every drop of blood drawn with the
lash, shall be paid by another drawn with
the sword, as was said three thousand years
ago, so still it must be said "the judgments
of the Lord, are true and righteous altogether"

        With malice toward none;
with charity for all; with firmness in the
right, as God gives us to see the right,
let us strive on to finish the work we
are in; to bind up the nation's wounds;
to care for him who shall have borne the battle, and for his widow, and his orphan—
to do all which may achieve and cherish a just
and a lasting peace, among ourselves, and with all nations.

by whom the offence came, shall we discern there-

in any departure from those divine attributes

which the believers in a Living God always

ascribe to Him? Fondly do we hope — fervent-

ly do we pray — that this mighty scourge of

war may speedily pass away. Yet, if God

wills that it continue, until all the wealth

piled by the bond-man's two hundred and

fifty years of unrequited toil shall be sunk,

                    of
and until every drop ∧ blood drawn with the

lash, shall be paid by another drawn with

the sword, as was said three thousand years

ago, so still it must be said "the judgments

of the Lord, arc true and righteous altogether"

        With malice toward none;

with charity for all; with firmness in the

right, as God gives us to see the right,

let us strive on to finish the work we

are in; to bind up the nation's wounds;
                        have
to care for him who shall ∧ borne the battle, and for his widow, and his orphan —
to do all which may achieve and cherish a just,
                                all nations.
and a lasting peace, among ourselves, and with ~~the world.~~

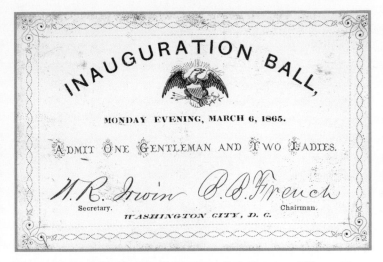

The 1865 inaugural ball was staged at the newly built Patent Office on F Street—now the National Portrait Gallery.

The inaugural ball menu—notwithstanding four years of war and deprivation—was typically sumptuous.

SECOND INAUGURAL ADDRESS, MARCH 4, 1865
Lincoln took this document, the product of typesetting and literal cutting and pasting,
with him to the dais at the U.S. Capitol. Notice how Lincoln's final emendation repeats the correction
made on the handwritten manuscript.

FELLOW COUNTRYMEN: At this second appearing to take the oath of the presidential office, there is less occasion for an extended address than there was at the first. Then, a statement, somewhat in detail, of a course to be pursued, seemed fitting and proper.

Now, at the expiration of four years, during which public declarations have been constantly called forth on every point and phase of the great contest which still absorbs the attention, and engrosses the energies of the nation, little that is new could be presented. The progress of our arms, upon which all else chiefly depends, is as well known to the public as to myself; and it is, I trust, reasonably satisfactory and encouraging to all. With high hope for the future, no prediction in regard to it is ventured.

On the occasion corresponding to this four years ago, all thoughts were anxiously directed to an impending civil war.

All dreaded it—all sought to avert it. While the inaugural address was being delivered from this place, devoted altogether to *saving* the Union without war, insurgent agents were in the city seeking to *destroy* it without war—seeking to dissolve the Union, and divide effects, by negotiation.

Both parties deprecated war; but one of them would *make* war rather than let the nation survive; and the other would *accept* war rather than let it perish.

And the war came.

One-eighth of the whole population were colored slaves, not distributed generally over the Union, but localized in the southern part of it. These slaves constituted a peculiar and powerful interest. All knew that this interest was, somehow, the cause of the war. To strengthen, perpetuate and extend this interest was the object for which the insurgents would rend the Union, even by war, while the government claimed no right to do more than to restrict the territorial enlargement of it. Neither party expected for the war, the magnitude, or the duration, which it has already attained.

Neither anticipated that the *cause* of the conflict might cease with, or even before, the conflict itself should cease. Each looked for an easier triumph, and a result less fundamental and astounding.

Both read the same Bible, and pray to the same God, and each invokes His aid against the other. It may seem strange that any men should dare to ask a just God's assistance in wringing their bread from the sweat of other men's faces; but let us judge not, that we be not judged. The prayers of both could not be answered—that of neither has been answered fully. The Almighty has His own purposes. "Woe unto the world because of offences! for it must needs be that offences come; but woe to that man by whom the offence cometh."

If we shall suppose that American slavery is one of those offences which, in the providence of God, must needs come, but which, having continued through His appointed time, He now wills to remove, and that He gives to both north and south this terrible war as the woe due to those by whom the offence came, shall we discern therein any departure from those divine attributes which the believers in a living God always ascribe to Him?

Fondly do we hope—fervently do we pray—that this mighty scourge of war may speedily pass away. Yet, if God wills that it continue until all the wealth piled by the bondman's two hundred and fifty years of unrequited toil shall be sunk, and until every drop of blood drawn with the lash, shall be paid by another drawn with the sword, as was said three thousand years ago, so still it must be said, "the judgments of the Lord are true and righteous altogether."

With malice toward none; with charity for all; with firmness in the right, as God gives us to see the right, let us strive on to finish the work we are in; to bind up the nation's wounds; to care for him who shall have borne the battle, and for his widow, and his orphan—to do all which may achieve and cherish, a just and a lasting peace, among ourselves, and with *all nations*.

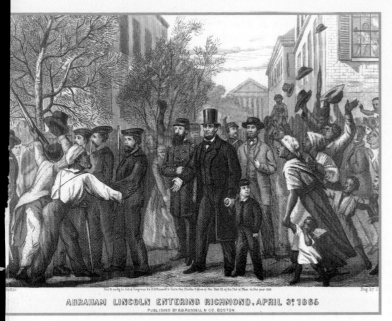

ABRAHAM LINCOLN ENTERING RICHMOND, APRIL 3ᵈ 1865
PUBLISHED BY B.B.RUSSELL & CO. BOSTON.

...th his young son Tad at his side, Lincoln visited the conquered Confederate capital ...Richmond, Virginia, on April 3, 1865—just twelve days before his death. The ...y's black population greeted him with affection and reverence. Artist L. Hollis's ...agined sketch of the scene was engraved the following year by J. C. Buttre.

...st weeks after his trip to Richmond, the country mourned Abraham Lincoln in ...is procession down Washington's Pennsylvania Avenue on April 19, 1865.

SVEN BIRKERTS

Consider two documents: the handwritten version of Lincoln's Second Inaugural, and the printed paste-up that served as his actual speaking text. Studied in juxtaposition they mark out segments of a line that begins in compositional privacy—words inscribed on the page by hand, preserving the suggestion of thought being shaped toward public cadence, but still also very clearly the product of one man's effort to impose deliberation on the surges of strong emotion. The printed text telegraphs not only the transformation of the private occasion into typographic public potential—the next point on the line—but in paste-up seems to convert the fluid nature of the first expression into a sequence to be tracked and performed, moving it not to the idea of speech, but to a speech, with all that that implies about strategy and persuasion. The idea of the line of course continues. We can then imagine the fragmented-looking paste-up, its discrete units of text, dissolving at the edges into impassioned delivery, gathering back to a unity of effect that preserves—possibly even amplifies—the quality of the original occasion, the spirit that first coaxed thoughts into sentences intended for an eventual public, if not for posterity. ◄

CONTRIBUTORS' BIOGRAPHIES

JONATHAN ALTER has worked in political commentary and media criticism in a variety of roles—as a columnist, critic, and senior editor for *Newsweek* magazine; a contributing correspondent at NBC News; a blogger for *The Huffington Post*; and author of a 2006 book, *The Defining Moment: Franklin Roosevelt and the First Hundred Days.*

SVEN BIRKERTS Essayist and literary critic Birkerts is the author of *The Gutenberg Elegies: The Fate of Reading in an Electronic Age* and *The Art of Time in Memoir: Then, Again,* a book of literary criticism on the theme of memoirs. He is the editor of the literary magazine *Agni,* a lecturer on nonfiction at Harvard University, and the director of the Bennington Writing Seminars at Bennington College.

DAVID W. BLIGHT Historian and educator Blight is a professor of history and director of the Gilder Lehrman Center for Slavery and Abolition at Yale University. His most recent book is *A Slave No More: Two Men Who Escaped to Freedom, Including Their Narratives of Emancipation.* He is on the board of advisors of the Abraham Lincoln Bicentennial Commission.

GABOR BORITT Fluhrer Professor of History at Gettysburg College, Boritt also directs its Civil War Institute and is cofounder and director of its annual Lincoln Prize. His many books include *Lincoln and the Economics of the American Dream* (1978) and *The Gettysburg Gospel* (2006). A native of Hungary, he was recently the subject of a documentary biography, filmed by his son Jake: *From Budapest to Gettysburg.*

BLISS BROYARD is the author of a book of stories (*My Father, Dancing*) and of a 2007 memoir of her discovery, as a young adult, of her father's mixed-race background. *One Drop: My Father's Hidden Life—A Story of Race and Family Secrets* explores the complex interactions among race, society, and individual choices.

MICHAEL BURLINGAME Historian Burlingame has written or edited many books on Lincoln, including 2007's *Abraham Lincoln: The Observations of John G. Nicolay and John Hay* and 2008's *Abraham Lincoln: A Life.* He is on the board of directors of the Abraham Lincoln Association and the Abraham Lincoln Institute.

KEN BURNS Emmy award–winning filmmaker and author Burns has directed and produced nearly two dozen documentaries, including *The Civil War*—which was, at the time, the most-watched historical documentary series ever on public television. Recently, he was the cocreator of the World War II documentary *The War* and coauthor of *The War: An Intimate History, 1941–1945.* Burns serves on the advisory committee for the Abraham Lincoln Bicentennial Commission.

PRESIDENT GEORGE H. W. BUSH served as the forty-first president of the United States, from 1989 to 1993, as well as, previously, vice president, director of the CIA, and chief of the U.S. Liaison Office in the People's Republic of China. He is the recipient of an honorary knighthood from Queen Elizabeth II.

PRESIDENT GEORGE W. BUSH served as the forty-third president of the United States, from 2001 to 2009, and as the forty-sixth governor of the State of Texas. He received degrees from Yale and Harvard and has published a memoir, *A Charge to Keep: My Journey to the White House.*

PRESIDENT JIMMY CARTER served as the thirty-ninth president of the United States, from 1977 to 1981. The former president founded the Carter Center, a nonprofit dedicated to furthering human rights and health, and leads the Jimmy and Rosalynn Carter Work Project for Habitat for Humanity International. Carter is a recipient of the Nobel Peace Prize.

PRESIDENT BILL CLINTON In his two terms as forty-second president of the United States, from 1993 to 2001, the former governor of Arkansas achieved a fiscal surplus from a huge national deficit. In 2001, President Clinton founded the William J. Clinton Foundation, whose programs focus on global issues, including climate change and health. He recently published *Giving: How Each of Us Can Change the World.*

MARIO M. CUOMO served as governor of New York from 1983 to 1995, was the co-editor of the 1993 book *Lincoln on Democracy* and author of the 2004 treatise *Why Lincoln Matters: Today More Than Ever.* He is currently counsel to the firm of Willkie Farr & Gallagher in New York and a member of the Advisory Council of the Abraham Lincoln Bicentennial Commission.

E. L. DOCTOROW Novelist Doctorow is a Glucksman Professor in American Letters at New York University and the recipient of the National Humanities Medal, among other awards. His literature often incorporates historical settings and figures. His 2005 novel *The March*, a Pulitzer Prize and National Book Award finalist, explores General William T. Sherman's movement through the southern states.

DAVID HERBERT DONALD Pulitzer Prize–winning historian Donald is the Charles Warren Professor of American History and Professor of American Civilization, Emeritus, at Harvard University. He is the author of a celebrated biography, *Lincoln*, and the recent *"We Are Lincoln Men": Abraham Lincoln and His Friends*, and has taught at Oxford University and Smith College, among others.

RICHARD J. DURBIN U.S. Senator Durbin of Illinois was elected Majority Whip of the Senate in 2006. He is one of the founding members of the Senate Global AIDS Caucus. He has received recognition from the American Lung Association, American Public Health Association, and others for his work in promoting more stringent public health legislation. He serves as cochairman of the U.S. Abraham Lincoln Bicentennial Commission.

DREW GILPIN FAUST Founding Dean of the Radcliffe Institute for Advanced Study, Faust is the first female president of Harvard University as well as Harvard's Lincoln Professor of History. A historian of the Civil War and the antebellum South, Faust is the author of six books, most recently *This Republic of Suffering: Death and the American Civil War*.

JENNIFER FLEISCHNER is the author of several works of historical fiction and biography, including *Mrs. Lincoln and Mrs. Keckley: The Remarkable Story of a Friendship Between a First Lady and a Former Slave*, that focus on the Civil War era and racial issues. She has served as the Chair of the English Department at Adelphi University and as a Mellon Faculty Fellow in Afro-American Studies at Harvard University.

JOHN HOPE FRANKLIN Distinguished historian and professor emeritus Franklin's bestselling book *From Slavery to Freedom: A History of African-Americans* has been in print since 1947. A recipient of the third John W. Kluge Prize for lifetime achievement in the humanities and of the Presidential Medal of Freedom, Franklin recently published *In Search of the Promised Land: A Slave Family in the Old South*.

HENRY LOUIS GATES, JR. Literary critic Gates's newest book is *In Search of Our Roots: How 19 Extraordinary African Americans Reclaimed Their Past*. He is the Alphonse Fletcher Jr. University Professor at Harvard University, the director of Harvard's W. E. B. Du Bois Institute for African and African American Research, and editor-in-chief of the online magazine *The Root*.

NEWT GINGRICH Former Speaker of the U.S. House of Representatives Gingrich is the recent founder and chair of the nonpartisan group American Solutions for Winning the Future and a senior fellow at the American Enterprise Institute. He is the author of many works of nonfiction and historical fiction, including *Gettysburg: A Novel of the Civil War*.

DORIS KEARNS GOODWIN Acclaimed historian Goodwin is most recently the author of *Team of Rivals: The Political Genius of Abraham Lincoln*. The Pulitzer Prize–winning author and former professor has written several bestsellers, each focusing on a U.S. president's life and times. She is also a news analyst for NBC.

ADAM GOPNIK Journalist Gopnik, recipient of three National Magazine Awards for essays and for criticism, and a George Polk Award for magazine reporting, has been writing essays for *The New Yorker* since 1986. His most recent book is *Angels and Ages: Lincoln, Darwin, and the Making of the Modern Age*.

PHILIP GOUREVITCH is the editor of *The Paris Review* and a staff writer for *The New Yorker*. His most recent book, *Standard Operating Procedure*, is an account of Iraq's Abu Ghraib prison. Gourevitch is also the author of *We Wish to Inform You That Tomorrow We Will Be Killed With Our Families*, which tells the story of the 1994 Rwandan Genocide, and *A Cold Case*, the story of an unsolved murder in New York City.

KATHRYN HARRISON is the author of many acclaimed works, including the novels *Envy*, *The Seal Wife*, *The Binding Chair*, *Poison*, *Exposure*, and *Thicker Than Water*; the memoirs *The Kiss*, *The Mother Knot*, and *The Road to Santiago*; and, most recently, *While They Slept: An Inquiry Into the Murder of a Family*. Her criticism and essays appear frequently in *The New York Times Book Review* and other publications.

TONY KUSHNER The winner of several awards (including a Pulitzer Prize, two Tony Awards, and an Emmy Award) for his writing for the stage and screen, playwright Kushner's most recent project is *Lincoln*—a biographical film about Abraham Lincoln, to be directed by Steven Spielberg. Kushner is the author of the acclaimed musical *Caroline, or Change* and the two-part play *Angels in America*.

LEWIS LEHRMAN founded the Lehrman Institute, a public policy research organization that includes the Lincoln Institute, devoted to encouraging the study of Abraham Lincoln. He also cofounded the Gilder Lehrman Center for Slavery and Abolition at Yale, and the Gilder Lehrman Institute of American History. Lehrman has worked prominently in the political and financial spheres, and in the humanities, focusing on American history. He received the National Humanities Medal in 2005.

THOMAS MALLON Former *GQ* editor and professor of English at Vassar College, Mallon is the author of numerous works of nonfiction and historical fiction, including his novel of the Lincoln Assassination, *Henry and Clara*. He is a member of the National Endowment for the Humanities' Advisory Board and a contributing writer to such publications as *The Atlantic Monthly*.

JAMES M. MCPHERSON A leading historian of the Civil War, McPherson is a Pulitzer Prize–winning and bestselling author of such landmark books as *Battle Cry of Freedom* and, most recently, *Tried by War: Abraham Lincoln as Commander-in-Chief*. McPherson is a professor emeritus at Princeton University and a member of the Lincoln Bicentennial Advisory Committee.

TONI MORRISON'S novels include *Sula, Song of Solomon, Beloved,* and *Paradise.* Her honors include the National Book Critics Circle Award, the Pulitzer Prize, and the Nobel Prize in Literature. She is the Robert F. Goheen Professor, Emerita, and special consultant to the director of the Princeton Atelier in the Lewis Center for the Arts at Princeton University.

WALTER MOSLEY has written over two dozen bestselling novels—particularly mysteries—and nonfiction books, including one on the potential role of African Americans in global peacekeeping. The critically acclaimed author has contributed to publications such as *The Nation* and *The New York Times Magazine.* He also helped create a publishing program at the City College of New York.

LIAM NEESON Academy Award–nominated Irish-born actor Neeson was cast to portray Abraham Lincoln in *Lincoln,* a film written by Tony Kushner and directed by Steven Spielberg. The stage and screen actor recently appeared in another film set in the Civil War era: 2007's *Seraphim Falls.* Neeson is also an Officer of the Order of the British Empire. He has read Lincoln's words at the Library of Congress.

CONAN O'BRIEN Emmy Award–winning comedic writer and television show host O'Brien has written for *The Simpsons* and *Saturday Night Live* and has hosted *Late Night With Conan O'Brien* since 1993. He will succeed Jay Leno as the host of *The Tonight Show* in 2009.

SANDRA DAY O'CONNOR The first female American Supreme Court Justice, O'Connor served on the court for twenty-four years. She has also written three books of memoirs. In 2006, O'Connor took part in the Iraq Study Group of the United States Institute of Peace. She is currently a chancellor of the College of William and Mary.

CYNTHIA OZICK has produced varied works of fiction and essays over several decades. Among her focuses are Jewish culture and history. Her critically acclaimed oeuvre includes *Heir to the Glimmering World* and *Metaphor and Memory.* She has received fellowships from the National Endowment for the Arts and the Guggenheim Foundation, among other awards.

ROBERT PINSKY served as Poet Laureate Consultant in Poetry to the Library of Congress from 1997 to 2000. His writing has won numerous awards, including a Guggenheim Foundation Fellowship. He founded the Favorite Poem Project, which documents and shares Americans' love for poetry, and is the poetry editor for the online magazine *Slate* and a professor at Boston University.

WILLIAM SAFIRE Currently the chairman of the Dana Foundation, and a journalist, columnist, and former presidential speechwriter, Safire has written on politics and language for *The New York Times* since the 1970s. He is also the author of *Freedom: A Novel of Abraham Lincoln and the Civil War.* In 2006, President George W. Bush awarded Safire the Presidential Medal of Freedom.

GEORGE SAUNDERS'S work includes the story collections *CivilWarLand in Bad Decline, Pastoralia,* and *In Persuasion Nation;* the novella *The Brief and Frightening Reign of Phil;* and the illustrated story *The Very Persistent Gappers of Frip,* with Lane Smith. His most recent book is *The Braindead Megaphone,* a collection of his satire and essays. A professor of creative writing at Syracuse University, Saunders is a four-time National Magazine Award winner and a 2006 MacArthur Fellow.

ANDREW SOLOMON is a contributing writer to *The New York Times Magazine* and a frequent contributor to *The New Yorker* as well as the author of award-winning essays and books, such as his acclaimed *The Noonday Demon: An Atlas of Depression.* He writes on diverse topics, including family, health, and psychology. Solomon has also been a member of the Council on Foreign Relations.

STEVEN SPIELBERG The internationally famous director and producer responsible for such films as *Jaws* and *Munich,* Spielberg is at work with playwright Tony Kushner on *Lincoln,* a biographical film about the sixteenth president. The three-time Academy Award winner recently received the French Légion d'honneur and is the recipient of a Cecil B. DeMille Award.

JOHN UPDIKE Prolific and much-honored fiction writer Updike is the recipient of both the National Medal of Arts and the National Medal for the Humanities and the author, most recently, of *Terrorist: A Novel* and *Due Considerations: Essays and Criticism.* Updike is a longtime contributor to *The New Yorker* and in the 1960s and 1970s worked as a cultural ambassador to the Soviet Union.

SAM WATERSTON Award-winning actor and humanitarian Waterston, well known for his role as Jack McCoy on NBC's *Law and Order* and for his highly esteemed stage and screen career, is a member of the Advisory Committee for the Lincoln Bicentennial. He portrayed Lincoln in the NBC miniseries *Lincoln* and read the words of Lincoln in Ken Burns's 1990 documentary *The Civil War,* and in many stage programs from the Library of Congress to the White House.

FRANK J. WILLIAMS Chief Justice of the Rhode Island Supreme Court, Williams is founding chairman of the Lincoln Forum, an organization whose activities unite people with an interest in Lincoln and the Civil War. He is also a member of the Lincoln Bicentennial Commission. Among his many books is a collection of essays on the sixteenth president, *Judging Lincoln.*

DOUGLAS L. WILSON Lincoln scholar Wilson is a professor emeritus and codirector of the Lincoln Studies Center at Knox College. He is the two-time recipient of the prestigious Lincoln Prize—most recently for his book *Lincoln's Sword: The Presidency and the Power of Words.*